THE
LITTLE
BOOK
OF THE

TUDORS

ANNIE BULLEN

The
History
Press

First published 2013
Reprinted 2016

The History Press
The Mill, Brimscombe Port
Stroud, Gloucestershire, GL5 2QG
www.thehistorypress.co.uk

British Library Cataloguing in Publication Data.
A catalogue record for this book is available from the British Library.

ISBN 978 0 7509 5575 1

Typesetting and origination by The History Press
Printed in India by Replika Press Pvt. Ltd.

CONTENTS

Introduction   5

1   Meet the Royals   7

2   At Work and Play   29

3   In Sickness and in Health   49

4   Friends and Foes   67

5   Feast and Famine   87

6   People and Places   103

7   Movers and Shakers   119

8   Keeping Up Appearances   141

9   Conclusion   157

    Further Reading   159

INTRODUCTION

he flamboyant, fanatical, extravagant and autocratic Tudors brought the greatest change to England since the Normans arrived in 1066.

Theirs was a comparatively short-lived dynasty; five monarchs, each markedly different in character from the other, ruled over the 118 years between 1485 and 1603. Dour, methodical and miserly Henry Tudor and his handsome son, the flamboyant Renaissance prince, Henry, Duke of York, who became something of a monster as he grew into kingship, established the dynasty. Priggish young Edward, intelligent and fervently Protestant, warred with his half-sister, the equally fervent Catholic 'Bloody Mary'. And Elizabeth, the Virgin Queen, Good Queen Bess, as extravagant as the rest, but cautious and clever enough to lay the foundations of a long and mostly peaceful rule.

But what of the ordinary people of England? The yeomen farmers and their busy wives, the wealthy merchants, the tradesmen and the labourers. How did they manage to make ends meet in those rapidly changing days? Where did they live? What did they eat and wear? How did they treat aches and pains and ailments? How did they amuse themselves in their leisure time?

This 'Little Book' gives you the low-down on the daily life of the ordinary people as well as vivid descriptions of the luxury in royal palaces. Compare the labourer's daily fare of basic 'pottage', a cabbage and vegetable soup, with a little meat if he was lucky, to the extravagance of a royal feast, composed of hundreds of elaborately dressed dishes, served over several hours. Read about Queen Elizabeth's two-hour dressing routine and contrast her gowns, kirtles, stomachers, stockings and jewels to the hastily assembled rough woollen gowns worn by the working women of her reign. What did a Tudor man wear under his doublet and hose? When would a Tudor elder call for a 'caudle' and how would he clean his teeth after eating it? Learn the difference between a garderobe and a 'close-stool' and find out why everyone, from the king downwards, feared the dreaded 'sweating sickness'.

1

Meet the Royals

n the freezing January of 1457 a 14-year-old girl, widowed and heavily pregnant, sought refuge at Pembroke Castle to give birth to a baby boy who would found a great dynasty that changed the shape of English monarchy.

The young woman, Margaret Beaufort, was an heiress, one of the richest in the country. Margaret, descended from John of Gaunt, had royal blood in her veins. She was cousin to the Lancastrian king, the weak and dangerously mad Henry VI, who had ordered her marriage, at the age of 12, to his half-brother, Edmund Tudor.

Edmund, the son of Catherine of Valois, Henry V's widowed queen, and Owen Tudor, a Welsh soldier and courtier, died in early November 1456,

Henry VII. (THP)

The late fifteenth century was a bloody, treacherous and dangerous time as England was torn asunder by a deadly civil tussle for the throne.

The warring Plantagenets, divided into Yorkist and Lancastrian factions, plunged the country into the Wars of the Roses, so called for their emblems – the white rose of York and the red of Lancaster, which their retainers wore as badges. The protagonists, abetted by wealthy supporters and their private armies, stopped at nothing in their bids to gain supremacy.

before his baby son was born. He had been more than twice his child-bride's age and their union was formed purely to provide a child as back-up to the Lancastrian succession of Henry VI. The birth, on 28 January 1457, of Henry Tudor, the future King Henry VII, eventually fulfilled those expectations, although, at the time, his claim to the throne was an obscure one.

EDWARD WINS THE THRONE FOR YORK

Margaret Beaufort's cousin, King Henry VI, was challenged and harried by Edward of York who, with his brothers, George, Duke of Clarence, and Richard, Duke of Gloucester, was descended, like Henry, from Edward III. The climax to this terrible struggle came in May 1471 when the bellicose Edward led his forces to massacre those of King Henry at Tewkesbury in Gloucestershire. The carnage was terrible, the battlefield strewn with thousands of Lancastrian bodies. Accounts at the time claim that those who escaped to ask for sanctuary in Tewkesbury Abbey were slaughtered by Edward and his henchmen. Henry's son, Edward, the Prince of Wales,

A contemporary description of Henry VII, written by Italian historian Polydore Vergil, describes the king as slender but well built and strong, and of average height: 'His appearance was remarkably attractive and his face was cheerful, especially when speaking; his eyes were small and blue, his teeth few, poor and blackish; his hair was thin and white; his complexion sallow.'

died too – some claim that he survived the battle only to be murdered by the Dukes of Clarence and Gloucester. His father, the king, fared no better. He was killed in the Tower of London, the back of his head smashed in, probably by Richard of Gloucester.

This is when life became dangerous for the 14-year-old Henry Tudor, Earl of Richmond. His shrewd mother, knowing that his claim to the throne would make him a marked man, ordered him to go into hiding in France.

Henry made for Brittany where he remained in exile for the next fifteen years, watching and waiting to return to his country to claim the Crown.

But there was trouble at home for the new King Edward IV; his brother George, the Duke of Clarence, who had proved to be an enthusiastic hit man while they were dispatching Lancastrians, had ambitions to be king himself. Between him and the throne were his brother and two nephews, Edward's sons by his wife, commoner Elizabeth Woodville. The boys, Edward and Richard, would be known later and throughout history as the Princes in the Tower. Now Clarence was spreading rumours that Edward's secret marriage to his queen was invalid – because he was already married to another woman at the time. If this were true, the two princes would be illegitimate and he, George, would be next in the line of succession.

Edward was furious and unforgiving. George was arrested on trumped-up charges, convicted and executed, as every history student knows, by drowning in a butt of malmsey wine in the Tower of London in January 1476.

❁ AN UNCLE'S TREACHERY ❁

Younger brother Richard, Duke of Gloucester, vowed loyalty, but when Edward died suddenly after contracting a fever in April 1483, he was swift and ruthless in his own bid to claim the throne.

He pushed his claim to be appointed 'Protector' of 12-year-old Prince Edward, heir and namesake of the dead king. The boy's mother, Elizabeth Woodville, fearing skulduggery, demanded that her son's coronation should be celebrated immediately, so Edward set out from his home in Ludlow Castle for London, to be crowned and to start his reign. But his escort of 2,000 men was intercepted

The murder of the Princes in the Tower. (THP)

Two influential mothers, each of whom had reason to hate King Richard, hatched the plot that united the warring factions of Lancaster and York and ended the Plantagenet dynasty.

Elizabeth Woodville, convinced that her boys had been murdered in the Tower by Richard, and Margaret Beaufort, whose son Henry was still in exile, waiting for the right time to claim the English throne, decided on a course of action that was to prove fatal to Richard. Elizabeth's daughter, also named Elizabeth, would marry Henry, bringing York and Lancaster together against the treacherous Richard III.

by Uncle Richard, whose regency or protectorship was confirmed. The young prince's coronation was put off and Edward was sent to live in the Tower of London, soon to be joined by his younger brother, Richard.

Just two months after the princes left Ludlow, parliament, directed by Richard, declared their father King Edward's marriage to Elizabeth Woodville invalid and the boys themselves bastards. Two weeks after that, on 6 July 1483, the date already set for young Edward's coronation, their uncle was crowned King Richard III at Westminster.

The boys were not seen again and by late summer even their grieving mother assumed that they were dead.

❂ HENRY'S BID FOR POWER ❂

Now Henry's chance to seize the throne from Richard had come. He was 30 years old and had lived in France for half of those years. Briefed by his mother and accompanied by a force of a couple of thousand French soldiers and a few hundred Englishmen, he landed at Milford Haven on 7 August 1485 and prepared to march through Wales,

Henry's own claim to legitimacy was open to challenge. His grandfather, Owen Tudor, a courtier, married the dowager queen Catherine of Valois in secret (although some historians claim that they were never married) and the couple had at least six children. Dowager queens were not allowed to remarry without royal permission so it could be claimed that the union was invalid and the children, including Henry VII's father, Edmund Tudor, illegitimate.

picking up some supporters as they moved relentlessly forward into England towards Bosworth in the Midlands. Trailing them were the vast and well-drilled soldiers of Lord Stanley, Margaret Beaufort's third husband, who was reluctant to commit to battle until he saw which way the wind was blowing for his stepson.

Richard's forces, attacking from the ridge, failed to break the much smaller front line of Henry's men. Richard and

The crown handed to Henry Tudor at Bosworth Field. (THP)

Henry, in the thick of it, fought face to face. Lord Stanley's men swept forward to help and Richard was killed, beaten so heavily that his helmet pierced his skull.

Lord Stanley stooped to retrieve the dead king's battered circlet from beneath a thorn bush and placed it on his stepson's head. Henry, Duke of Richmond, the exile, was now King Henry VII, the first Tudor King of England.

❀ THE DAWN OF A DYNASTY ❀

At Henry's coronation in Westminster Abbey at the end of October 1485, the new king was reunited with his mother, Lady Margaret Beaufort. Neither had seen the other for fourteen years, but each knew that the way ahead would be tough. Royal dynasties relied on large family clans, vast acres and private armies. Henry had none of these and he knew that the spectre of civil war loomed over the early part of his reign.

But a few months after the coronation the marriage between him and Elizabeth of York took place, thus uniting the rival factions and giving authority to his claim to legitimacy. The white and red roses, emblems that had signified war, now were fused into the red and white Tudor rose, symbolising his intent to bring unity.

Hollar's seventeenth-century view of London showing Westminster Abbey, where Henry VII was crowned, on the right. (With kind permission of the Thomas Fisher Rare Book Library, University of Toronto)

Skirmishes with the French and some attempts by imposters claiming the throne were dealt with before Henry settled down to create his dynasty and build royal finances in a way that curbed the power of the barons and aristocratic clans, as well as providing revenue for the defence of the realm. He banned private armies which had allowed the great landowners of England to rise up in rebellion and he issued bonds, which were to be forfeit in the event of bad behaviour.

He and his Lord Chancellor, the lawyer-clergyman John Morton, devised fiendish taxes. Morton reasoned that those who spent lavishly were obviously rich enough to pay, while the frugal must have money tucked away to give to the king. Thus the expression 'Morton's Fork' – being caught between two unpleasant choices – was coined.

Gradually the Tudor monarchy was secured and became entrenched. His heraldic devices, the Tudor rose, portcullises, greyhounds and the red dragon of Wales, symbols of the dynasty – the 'branding' of the Tudor name – were painted

Henry and Elizabeth harked back to a more chivalrous and romantic age when planning the birth of their first child. Gambling that it would be a boy, the king remembered that the mythical Merlin had said that the legendary King Arthur was the son of a red king and a white queen. So Prince Arthur was born at Winchester Castle (Winchester was, in legend, Camelot) in the early hours of 20 September 1486. Outriders galloped the length and breadth of the nation to spread the good news, great fires were lit in celebration and minstrels sung a new lay: 'Joyed may we be, Our prince to see, and roses three' – referring to the red and white roses of Lancaster and York and the new Tudor emblem, a rose of both colours.

on his gatehouses and palaces, shields and liveries. He created his own bodyguard – a 300-strong, hand-picked force known as the Yeomen of the Guard.

Soon the succession looked secure with the birth of Henry and Elizabeth's first child, a son whom they named Arthur.

❖ DEATH OF A PRINCE ❖

However, the tenuous security was shattered with the terrible news that arrived on 4 April 1502, as night fell at Greenwich, where Henry and Elizabeth were in residence. Their beloved Arthur, just 15 and newly married to the Spanish *infanta* Catherine of Aragon, had died in his room at Ludlow Castle, stricken with the lethal flu-like sweating sickness which had swept the country. Henry and Elizabeth were distraught. Arthur was their future, the heir to the English throne, their young prince in whom so much had been invested. Only five months earlier, London had been alive for days with the most lavish celebrations for the wedding of the two young royals who had moved to Arthur's Welsh castle after the ceremonies.

Arthur was buried three weeks later with impressive pomp at Worcester Cathedral. The future of the Tudor line now depended on the 10-year-old Duke of York, Prince Henry, who had been brought up by his mother at Greenwich Palace and nearby Eltham Manor with his sisters, Margaret and Mary, while his older brother was being groomed for kingship.

More tragedy hit the Royal Family less than a year later. Henry Tudor's wife, Elizabeth, who had comforted him on Arthur's death by promising to bear another child and who he loved and respected, died on her thirty-seventh birthday, 11 February 1503. She had gone into confinement in the Tower of London to give birth to the promised baby, when she developed a raging fever which could not be cured. The baby, a sickly girl, hastily christened Catherine, lived only a few hours.

Elizabeth of York, Henry's wife, and Margaret Beaufort, his pushy mother, could not have been more different but each was a key figure in the Tudor king's life. Elizabeth was beautiful, calm and serene, counselling and reconciling where there was strife and gracious in all situations. Margaret Beaufort, always at her daughter-in-law's elbow, tried to manage her as she had her son. She was a pious moraliser and a suspicious employer, forever seeking out the sins of servants rather than appreciating their good qualities. Her legacy, however, is considerable. She established the Lady Margaret Professorship of Divinity at the University of Cambridge in 1502 and three years later refounded Christ's College, Cambridge. Her death saw the foundation, in 1509, of Wimborne Grammar School (now Queen Elizabeth's School) and, in 1511, of St John's College, Cambridge.

Henry and Elizabeth's marriage of convenience had become a partnership of real love and mutual comfort. The death of the still-young queen shattered not only her husband, who had relied on her in so many matters, but also had a deep impact on her son, Henry, whose carefree childhood was now at an end.

After Elizabeth's death, Henry Tudor withdrew into himself, spending more time in his privy chamber, obsessively checking his accounts. By the time he died in 1509, rich and miserly, his subjects were ready to welcome their new young king, 17-year-old Henry VIII. The glorious Crown Imperial, commissioned twenty years earlier by his father and richly encrusted with colourful and glittering precious stones, was placed on the new king's head at Westminster Abbey on 24 June 1509. The nation rejoiced, full of hope for a blossoming of Tudor England

Henry VIII. (With kind permission of the Thomas Fisher Rare Book Library, University of Toronto)

under this idealistic, chivalrous and romantic young man whose happy nature seemed so different from that of his money-obsessed father.

❀ COURT OF A NEW KING ❀

Henry's road to rulership was paved with the highest ideals of courtly chivalry. His mother, responsible for his education, had provided him with first-rate tutors, but had also instilled in him tales of the legendary King Arthur and the history of Henry V, whose military prowess brought him dazzling victory over the French at Agincourt.

So the young king, fired with desire to restore the English reputation as conquering heroes, set up a brilliant court where martial arts, jousting and tournaments, with all their glamour and pageantry, held central place. And Henry made it his business to excel in these war games, as he did hunting and hawking. His kingship was glorious and visible to all – and all admired this brilliant, athletic and handsome young man. Sir Thomas More wrote: 'There is fiery power in his eyes, beauty in his cheeks as is typical of roses.' Who then could have imagined Henry in later life, crippled with obesity, ulcerous and barely able to walk?

The Spanish alliance against the old enemy, France, was re-formed as Henry married Catherine, his brother's widow. He had the money, thanks to his father, and he had the military skill to take on the French when they threatened to depose the pope, so in 1513 he was at the head of an English army crossing the Channel to join forces with the pope's soldiers to give the French a good drubbing and to take a couple of cities.

English military reputation restored and honour satisfied, Henry returned home and began the lifelong quest that bought him his place in history – the safe birth of a healthy legitimate son who would carry on the Tudor name. That quest was to see him not only marry six wives but also shift the monarchy from being part of an intercontinental dynasty, owning land and allegiance across Europe, to a nation state with the sovereign at the head of the armed forces, parliament and the Church. Henry broke with Rome and the pope, putting himself at the head of the English Church and paving the way for the Protestant religion which he had spent much of his life suppressing.

Henry and Catherine's daughter, Mary, was born safely in 1516 after a miscarried daughter and three sickly boy babies who lived only a short while. Nevertheless, it seemed that there was still plenty of time for the queen to conceive a son. But after one more pregnancy

The flamboyant Thomas Wolsey, the bright son of an Ipswich butcher, rose to become Henry's administrator and hit man, dealing with the tedious day-to-day business of running the country and organising military campaigns. Wolsey, as pleasure-seeking as the king himself, knew how to flatter and cajole but also how to get things done. He rose from royal chaplain to Bishop of Lincoln and then on to Archbishop of York before being made a cardinal and Lord Chancellor of England. Wolsey's great palace at Hampton Court is testament to his power and influence. He created his own legend with an infallible sense of drama and display. But for all his cleverness, he was unable to secure Henry's divorce from his first wife Catherine, and had he not died at Leicester Abbey on his way to London to face a charge of treason in 1530, it seems certain he would have lost his head on the executioner's block.

Old allegorical print of Henry VIII trampling the pope. (THP)

that brought a short-lived daughter, the king's eye fell elsewhere. He had had mistresses and one acknowledged illegitimate son, but by 1525 he was in love with one of Catherine's ladies-in-waiting, the dark-eyed, raven-haired Anne, daughter of Thomas Boleyn, Earl of Wiltshire. Anne's sister, Mary, was one of Henry's mistresses but the ambitious Anne wanted more – she was determined to become Henry's wife and Queen of England.

❁ QUEST FOR AN HEIR ❁

Anne achieved her aim by refusing to sleep with Henry until they could marry. The road to divorce and remarriage was a long and tumultuous one but eventually, in January 1533, the wedding took place in secret, despite the fact that Catherine was still legally his wife. Anne had finally given in to Henry and was pregnant. In May Archbishop Thomas Cranmer, defying the pope, ruled that Henry's marriage to Catherine was invalid (incidentally making their daughter, Mary, a bastard) and his marriage to Anne legal.

In September a daughter, Elizabeth, was born and, although Henry professed to be a doting father, he was becoming desperate for a son. By 1536, after three miscarriages, Anne's hold over the king had disappeared and he was in love again – this time to the mouse-like Jane Seymour. Anne had to go, and her dispatch at the hands of the executioner on charges of witchcraft, incest and adultery with several alleged lovers, including her brother George Boleyn, was swift and cruel.

Less than two weeks later, Henry and Jane Seymour were married and at last a son, Edward, was born. But poor Jane died days after the baby's birth in October 1537.

Henry had his male heir but, not content, he needed a 'spare' and looked abroad, to Flanders, for wife number four. But when Henry was unable or unwilling to consummate the marriage with Anne of Cleves (dubbed 'the Flanders mare')

Hollar's engraving of a portrait of Catherine Howard.
(With kind permission of the Thomas Fisher Rare Book
Library, University of Toronto)

an annulment was arranged and the quest was on again for
a suitable wife of child-bearing age.

Anne Boleyn's teenage cousin, Catherine Howard, might
have been flattered to have been chosen as the king's fifth
wife but by this time Henry, almost 50, horribly obese and

with ulcerated legs, was not the most romantic of figures. The inevitable followed her adultery and she was executed in 1542.

Henry VIII and his wives. Clockwise from top: Anne of Cleves; Catherine Howard; Anne Boleyn; Catherine of Aragon; Catherine Parr; Jane Seymour. (THP)

Henry's last wife, the sensible and comforting Catherine Parr, produced no children, but she helped him restore relations with his daughters and achieve some domestic happiness.

Before he died in 1547, Henry made his will, setting out the order in which his children, including his two daughters, were to succeed him. But he went to his grave still trying to tread a middle way through the religious muddle he had created. He continued to hold dear the ceremonies of the old church that he grew up with, while flatly denying the power of the pope. His children would, in turn, impose different forms of religion on a confused England.

❂ THE CLEVER BOY-KING ❂

Precociously clever at the age of 9, when he succeeded, Henry's longed-for son, able to conduct serious discussions in French and Latin, was guided by a council and protectors. The Duke of Somerset, his uncle, and later the Earl of Warwick both favoured radical Protestantism and imposed this form of religion. Edward embraced religious reform and endorsed the destruction of church ornaments and decoration – stained glass, crucifixes and wall paintings were all stripped away. Superstitious rituals such as Easter processionals, saints' day celebrations and pilgrimages were banned, as were hospitals, colleges and schools, paid for by benefactors who believed that providing these institutions for the benefit of the needy would speed their souls' passage to heaven. The Book of Common Prayer, written by Archbishop Cranmer, was introduced, while Mass was henceforth said in English.

Edward's relationship with his half-sister Mary, a devout Catholic, was strained to breaking point, especially as she insisted on celebrating the Roman Mass; only her royal position saved her from imprisonment.

PARVVLE PATRISSA. PATRIS. VIRTVTIS ET HÆRES
ESTO, NIHIL MAIVS MAXIMVS ORBIS HABET,
GRATVM VIX POSSVNT COELVM ET ATVRA DEDISSE,
HVIVS QVEM PATRIS. VICTVS HONORET HONOS.
ÆQVATO TANTVM. TANTI TV FACTA PARENTIS,
VOTA HOMINVM. VIX QVO PROGREDIANTVR, HABENT
VINCITO VICISTI. QVOT REGES PRISCVS ADORAT
ORBIS. NEC TE QVI VINCERE POSSIT. ERIT.

Hollar's engraving of a portrait of Edward VI, Henry VIII's son. (With kind permission of the Thomas Fisher Rare Book Library, University of Toronto)

Edward became seriously ill, probably from tuberculosis, and died in 1553, aged 15, having done his best to ensure that his father's will was ignored and that Lady Jane Grey, a fervent Protestant and the great-granddaughter of Henry VII, should inherit the Crown. But Mary Tudor acted decisively, raising an army to march to London, where she was proclaimed queen by the Privy Council on 19 July 1553.

Lady Jane, having acted as de facto queen for just nine days, was sent to the Tower and later executed for treason.

◉ 'BLOODY' MARY ◉

Mary promised moderation but, the rebellion defeated and her half-sister, the Protestant Elizabeth, sent to the Tower, she set about restoring the old faith. First she had to provide an heir and to that end she married the Spanish Prince Philip, son of Emperor Charles V, ruler of the Holy Roman Empire. They married at Winchester Cathedral on 25 July 1554 and soon Mary declared herself pregnant and began the serious and terrible business of ridding the country of those who denied the Catholic faith.

For three years cruel fires blazed, burning Protestant men and women alive at the stake. Bloody Mary, as the queen became known, retired to Hampton Court to bear the child who would take forward the Catholic England that she was restoring. But by summer 1555 it became obvious that Mary's pregnancy was a delusion, a phantom. With the fading of her hopes for an heir and the disappearance of her husband to Europe came a diminution of her authority. Mary became seriously ill in 1558, although she declared her indisposition was the result of another pregnancy. No one believed her and she died in November at the age of 42, leaving the way clear for her half-sister Elizabeth, now living at Hatfield House, to succeed.

◉ TREADING THE MIDDLE GROUND ◉

Just 25 and already politically astute when she became queen in 1558, Elizabeth, after being released from the Tower and living at Hatfield, was expecting news of Mary's death. The story that she knelt on the ground, piously exclaiming, 'This is the Lord's doing; it is marvellous in our eyes!' may or may not be true, but the quotation, from Psalm 118, was apt in her situation.

A contemporary description of Elizabeth calls her 'a lady of great elegance both of body and mind, although her face may rather be called pleasing than beautiful; she is tall and well-made; her complexion fine, though rather sallow, her eyes, and above all her hands, which she takes care not to conceal, are of superior beauty'.

Now, helped by her friend and mentor the Protestant Sir William Cecil, Baron Burghley, who became her Secretary of State, Elizabeth set out to create a moderate Protestant religious settlement. She endorsed the Act of Uniformity which restored the independence of an English Protestant Church, of which she, as monarch, became the Supreme Governor. This church later evolved into the Church of England.

Catholic plots persisted, especially after the pope excommunicated the queen in 1570, authorising Catholics to overthrow and even murder her. But these conspiracies to take her life were defeated, rooted out by her efficient 'secret service' under her principal secretary, Sir Francis Walsingham. Elizabeth moved cautiously, using her motto *video et taceo* ('I see and say nothing') as a mantra.

Throughout her forty-five-year reign, pressure on Elizabeth to marry and provide heirs was often intense, but here she played a long game. History says that the love of her life was her childhood friend Robert Dudley,

Elizabeth was her father's daughter, enjoying hunting, gambling, dancing and other sports. In the freezing winter of 1564–65 the ice on the Thames brought people out to play games on the frozen river. Queen Elizabeth ordered her courtiers out on to the slippery surface so that she and they might enjoy a round or two of archery.

Robert Dudley, Earl of Leicester. (THP)

her Master of the Horse, but although marriage might have been discussed, it never happened. The court rumour machine had it that Dudley's wife, Amy (*née* Robsart), was seriously ill (probably suffering from breast cancer) and that the queen would favour him as a husband should his wife die. Then, in September 1560, Amy Dudley was found dead, with a broken neck and head wounds, at the foot of stairs at her Oxfordshire home. An inquest verdict of 'accidental death' did nothing to quell the rumours that the accident was nothing of the sort. Elizabeth certainly considered marriage with Dudley, who she made Earl of Leicester, but her closest councillors advised her against it, warning of a likely rebellion if the marriage happened. When she died, among her most treasured possessions was a note from him on which she had written 'his last letter'.

❀ COUSINS AT WAR ❀

In 1568 Elizabeth's cousin, the Catholic Mary Queen of Scots, forced to flee Scotland, sought refuge in London and became the focus for militant Catholics seeking to depose Elizabeth. Mary was imprisoned but Elizabeth seemed reluctant to sign a death warrant. When a letter from Mary condoning a plot to murder Elizabeth was intercepted, the warrant was signed but recalled by the English sovereign, until, eventually, it was sent behind Elizabeth's back, to salve her conscience at the execution of a royal relative.

Elizabeth's time of glory came when her half-sister Bloody Mary's widower, Phillip II, sent the Spanish Armada to restore Catholic might to England and to seek revenge for acts of piracy against Spanish ships by English seamen. The Spanish fleet was famously defeated by the English navy (aided by the weather) and the nation's mood lifted, while Elizabeth's standing was at an all-time high in the eyes of her people.

The so-called Virgin Queen reigned for forty-five years, giving a time of peace and stability when culture and exploration flourished; William Shakespeare, Christopher Marlowe, Thomas Kyd, Thomas Middleton, John Fletcher and Francis Beaumont wrote for the theatre, while men like Sir Francis Drake, Sir Walter Raleigh, Sir John Hawkins and Sir Richard Grenville explored the world's seas, bringing trade and riches home to queen and country in what has been seen by some as a golden age. But Elizabeth went to her grave childless, the Tudor dynasty dying with her.

2

AT WORK
AND PLAY

veryone loves a royal wedding and that was as true in the early sixteenth century as now.

The importance of the occasion was matched by its entertainment value; huge crowds jostled to watch the colourful pomp and pageantry that lasted days.

In Tudor times a vast amount depended on the alliance between two great houses strengthening links between each other to act as partners in times of war and to foster trade during peace.

Henry Tudor's son, Arthur, was betrothed to Catherine of Aragon, daughter of the Spanish king and queen, Ferdinand and Isabella, by proxy in 1499, but it wasn't until Catherine finally arrived in England in November 1501 that the whole of London was entertained by a glittering display of pageantry and showmanship to celebrate the wedding. The 15-year-old princess, travelling on mule-back, was met by gorgeously apparelled knights and nobles, jewels glinting and plumed headdresses moving in the late autumn breeze. Riding at their head was Arthur's younger brother, Prince Henry, Duke of York, in his crimson cloak, attended by 100 liveried retainers, their tawny and blue uniforms brightening the dull day.

Catharine of Aragon, from a miniature by Holbein. (THP)

Henry, just 10, but already a self-possessed showman, escorted his brother's bride to London Bridge, where they were joined by the scarlet-gowned mayor and his two dozen aldermen over the lowered drawbridge into the square. Here was built the first of a series of magnificent tableaux to welcome the Spanish princess to her new life.

Catherine's attendants caused a stir among onlookers. The exotic strangers, gloriously liveried, were black Africans – the first to be seen by many English people. One of these servants was John Blanke, a talented musician who later became part of King Henry VIII's court.

⬡ ROYAL ENTERTAINMENT ⬡

The royal procession moved between houses hung with costly fabrics and tapestries, cloth of gold, satins and velvets as they wended their way towards the city, stopping along the route to marvel at a series of elaborate tiered stages offering tableaux each more dramatic and colourful than the other.

Onlookers pressed forward to catch a glimpse of the Spanish princess, remarking how small she seemed as she rode, straight-backed, on her mount, her long auburn hair set off by a deep red hat, framing her pale, snub-nosed face. Everywhere were cheering crowds following the party to the eastern gate of St Paul's churchyard, where Catherine received gifts of gold and plate before entering the cathedral for a blessing and thanksgiving.

There were still two days to go before the marriage but festivities continued through to the wedding day with its own sumptuous feasting and ceremony. The newlywed teenagers were given a day's respite from the public rejoicing before the entertainments resumed with ever-increasing magnificence for a whole week. Londoners were thrilled by the staged jousting in Westminster Palace yard and a glorious royal river procession, while in the evening there were plays, pageants, feasting, music and dancing in Westminster Hall. Then came another river journey when the royal barges – the king's, with its red dragon prow, in their midst – set off upriver to Henry VII's luxurious house at Richmond. Musicians with their recorders, tabors and trumpets accompanied them and their attendant flotilla of sixty boats on the 8-mile journey to the ultra-modern red-brick palace which boasted running water, glittering glass windows

Henry's most showy piece for the wedding celebrations was a triumph of design. Replacing the usual celebratory wine fountain flowing to keep the crowds happy outside St Paul's on the wedding day, his carpenters and decorators built an artificial mountain, green and glittering with precious metal. This was his 'rich mount', enhanced by three trees on its summit, each shading an armour-clad king. The central tree, belonging to King Arthur, was covered with red roses and sheltered a fierce red dragon. Scores of people wound around the fantastic edifice to fill their cups with the wine that poured without cease from the heart of the 'mountain'.

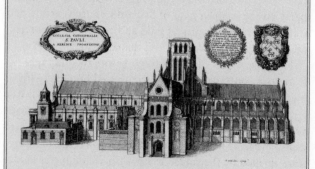

St Paul's Cathedral (south side). (With kind permission of the Thomas Fisher Rare Book Library, University of Toronto)

It is hard to equate the value of Tudor money with that of today's because the worth of individual goods and services has changed over the centuries. However, the average wage of a skilled Tudor labourer or craftsman, such as a carpenter or a stonemason, was between 4*d* and 10*d* a day – in the days when there were 144*d* in the pound. In the first quarter of the twenty-first century, payment for an equivalent day's work would be around £120 a day.

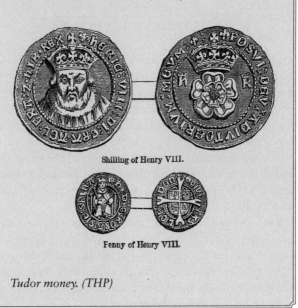

Shilling of Henry VIII.

Penny of Henry VIII.

Tudor money. (THP)

and sumptuous furnishings. During the day the guests wandered in the glorious gardens where trees were clipped into the fantastical shapes of mythical beasts. They passed the time playing chess, cards, dice or 'tables' (backgammon), practising archery, bowling or tennis, or simply enjoying the sight of Henry's red roses, evident everywhere, inside and outside the palace.

The magnificent entertainment finally ended on the evening of 28 November with the release, in the great hall at Richmond, of a flock of white doves, signifying peace and prosperity.

But entertainment of this sort was a spectator sport only for the majority of the king's subjects, whose own leisure activities were much more humble.

Each strata of society enjoyed its own pleasures, many of which were banned to the humblest (and poorest).

❁ MAKING A LIVING ❁

Tudor England encompassed a society rigid in its structure. At its head was the monarch and then the nobility. But there were not too many nobles because Tudor sovereigns from Henry VII, conscious that they wanted to limit the power of those below them, created few new barons, earls, marquesses or viscounts to challenge their total authority. Incomes of the remaining nobility varied, with the few richest garnering more than £10,000 a year but most averaging between £3,000 and £5,000.

Even on these huge sums many found that the necessary pleasures of life – hunting and hawking, buying fine clothes and jewels, eating and drinking, and forking out for expensive mistresses – put them into debt. But, unlike the poorer classes, noblemen could not be imprisoned for running up bills they could not pay.

If noblemen were thin on the ground, by far the most influential class in England was the 'gentry' – those knights and gentlemen who had enough income generated from their property not to have to earn a living in any other way. Landed gentlemen included those with great estates bringing in up to £4,000 per annum, to those living comfortably off the £200–£300 income earned each year by letting out their acres to tenant farmers.

Some of the richest in the country, with incomes running to more than £10,000, were the London merchants, grown wealthy through astute trading – often associated with buying and selling wool which was the fabric of life in Tudor England, used for making fine materials and the clothes worn by all, as well as furnishings and blankets. These men wielded political influence, too, becoming aldermen or heading one of the great livery companies.

The gentry were the backbone of England. It was from their ranks that the justices of peace, who sat as magistrates in their home counties, were drawn. Not only were they assiduous in choosing their representatives in the House of Commons, but many of them were chosen as Members of Parliament themselves.

Ambitious and clever men could train and work hard in one of the three professions that demanded a university degree. Clergymen, lawyers and physicians were all respected and, while senior members of the first two professions (archbishops, some bishops and many lawyers) could reckon on a good income in the low thousands, a canon or dean would have to be content with between £50–£450 per annum and a country rector £30.

Doctors were not always held in high regard and their incomes were way below those of their legal or ecclesiastical neighbours.

Other traders found life a struggle. Some shopkeepers made just enough to keep their businesses afloat and their families fed, while those wanting to set up a business or trade normally had to be accepted as legitimate craftsmen by their communities.

Most cities demanded that a businessman – someone with a trade who wanted to practise it – should become a freeman of that city and should gain this honour by being

Everyday needs were met by a huge variety of craftsmen or traders, all of whom had to become freemen of their towns or cities before they could trade. They varied from butchers and bakers, furriers, hosiers and gunners to bookbinders, masons, carpenters, clothiers, glovers, goldsmiths and felt makers. There were hoopers and parchment makers, milliners and millers, shuttle makers, innkeepers, locksmiths, ostlers and many more besides.

the son of one such, by serving a long apprenticeship or by buying his way in with a 'fine', of anything from £1 to £5. That amount was hard to find on a skilled labourer's wage; men such as masons, carpenters, felt makers or coopers earned between 4d and 10d a day, depending on whether they were given food and drink as part of their wages.

Yeomen lived in the country and worked on their farms, often employing labourers to help them. A yeoman, while not pretending to be a gentleman (who also farmed, but in name only, leasing or renting the land to others who did the hard work), would often earn more money than a gentleman.

Rural craftsmen and labourers took what work there was. If a man had a craft such as basket making, brewing, shoeing horses, thatching, knife-sharpening, wheel making or crafting hurdles, he would ply it when he could, often taking a labouring job when extra hands were needed at harvest time. He might live in a tiny cottage with rights to graze cattle or horses on common land and he would probably grow what he could in his own small garden to provide a little extra for his family.

❁ WOMEN'S WORK ❁

Although many upper-class Tudor women were as well educated as their male counterparts, the lot of most female members of society was to be regarded as the chattel of the male head of the household. So a father, male relative or husband determined what happened to property owned by a woman, or of the disposal of any income she might have.

She could not vote, become a magistrate or a lawyer, although she could obtain a licence to become a surgeon – something that rarely happened. Women were also allowed to take up the unpaid post of churchwarden but, again, few did.

Marriage meant transferring obedience from father to husband but, despite the restrictive laws and practices, many married middle-class women had satisfying, if busy, lives. In those times of largely self-sufficient households, they and their servants had to see to it that bread was baked and that beer was brewed. This was the drink of choice for men, women and children in times when it was not safe to drink water. There was meat to be cured, bacon and hams to be salted, fruit and vegetables to be pickled, preserved and turned into jams and jellies (if the household could afford to buy sugar) for the long winter months. Wool was spun into cloth, which was in turn made into clothes for the family.

Lower down the social order, farmers' wives milked the cows, made butter and cheese, kept fowls for meat and eggs, bees for their honey and grew fruit, herbs and vegetables which they might take to market to sell.

Medical help was expensive and Tudor wives learnt how to treat illnesses, brewing up a 'simple' or herbal remedy to ease fevers, colds, aches and pains.

Women were not allowed to become freemen of towns and cities; therefore, entering a trade or setting themselves up as craftswomen was not possible. But women could, and did, work in their husbands' businesses, often keeping the accounts and, in the event of the man's death, the widow would have been allowed to carry on the trade, so that she could support the family.

Plenty of women helped their husbands run taverns. They were known as 'ale-wives' and very often, if they were widowed, would carry on running the alehouse as before. Women could become licensed midwives and many did, while older women, often widowed, would

Washerwomen at work. (THP)

become carers for the sick, earning a comparatively good wage (but risking death themselves) cooking and cleaning for plague victims whose houses, and all therein, were automatically boarded up for six weeks whether the sick perished or recovered. The helper could ask for 6s 8d a week, which would go a long way if she survived. The word 'nurse' was used only for the wet nurses who fed rich women's infants, but these carers would travel

Tudor women had to be brave. Many marriages were those of convenience and a wife had to resign herself to the knowledge that all the household chores would fall to her. Tudor men did not cook or clean. Childbirth was a painful and dangerous time, and the mother knew that a quarter of all children born would die before their tenth birthday. If a husband was displeased, no one would intervene if he beat his wife – this was seen as perfectly normal as long as he did not kill her in the process.

Nevertheless, many marriages – especially in better-off households and those where women had an education equal to that of their husband – were long and fruitful. European observers noticed at the time that prosperous married English women had more freedom than their counterparts across the Channel. If they had servants to see to the drudgery, they were able to leave the house and household tasks to visit friends, play cards and socialise. They were treated with the utmost courtesy and were served first when banqueting and dining out with their husbands.

Tudor times saw the first English queens, Mary and Elizabeth, ruling in their own right and also the publication of work by educated women and female scholars.

around villages, helping the sick by washing and feeding them, sitting by the bedside and perhaps applying some of the dubious and often gruesome remedies listed in medical journals of the time. These often included ingredients such as crushed worms, chicken brains, turpentine and seaweed pounded, boiled and mashed to make healing decoctions. One remedy recommended using the 'dags', or unwashed wool, from between a sheep's back legs.

Payment for general care was less, but enough, at between 4d and 6d a day or night, to live off.

Others became washerwomen or laundresses, a job that was hard work and tough on the hands. Plenty of hot water, a capacious tub, a scrubbing board and soap were the tools of the trade. Some made their own soap from ashes, lye or lime, and a lot of animal tallow or fat. If this seemed too difficult, soap could be bought, ranging from the very basic cheap black product to a rather better grey soap made from potash and tallow, but still foul-smelling. These soaps cost around 1d a pound. About three times more expensive, but much more pleasant to handle, were the cakes of hard white Castile soap, which had to be used for fine white linen as the cheaper varieties would turn it black or grey. The charge for laundering a good linen shirt was 1d. Tudor men, however lowly in status, would not have dreamed of doing anything so demeaning as scrubbing clothes – cleaning was always women's work.

❀ NO PLACE FOR THE POOR ❀

One class of people did badly in Tudor England. The poor were certainly always evident, as vagrants, beggars or simply the old and sick. There was little or no provision for these people until 1563, in the early years of Queen Elizabeth's reign, when a Poor Law required townspeople

Beggars. (With kind permission of the Thomas Fisher Rare Book Library, University of Toronto)

to pay a levy towards the upkeep of the poverty-stricken. A decade later, plans were made to find paid work for the poor and, in 1597, a new Act appointed overseers in every parish to help the children of the poor, to find work for those who were not supporting themselves and to raise taxes in order to provide further support. Cruel punishment and hounding of the poor was banned and workhouses were established to give a place of shelter and to prevent the practice of persecuting the poor until they were forced to rob or steal so that they found themselves at the end of a hangman's rope.

❀ TIME OFF ❀

Just as today, Tudor men and women loved a day off or a night out. Music, dancing, drinking with good conversation and perhaps a flirtation to liven things up were to everybody's taste.

The rich would have enjoyed all these pleasures at a banquet or feast, while the ordinary men and women went to taverns and alehouses where a fiddler or a piper played as they knocked back ale or sipped sweet wine.

Guests at Henry VIII's table not only enjoyed a royal spread, they might be entertained by one or more of the fifty-eight musicians he retained, playing

Queen Elizabeth loved to dance and, so John Stanhope of her Privy Chamber reported, used it to keep fit. In 1589, when Elizabeth was in her mid-50s, he wrote, 'the Queen is so well as I assure you, six or seven galliards in a morning, besides music and singing, is her ordinary exercise.' Her half-sister Queen Mary had closed all London's dancing schools but, when they opened again during Elizabeth's reign, they – or the various Italian dancing masters in the city – had no shortage of clients desperate to perfect their steps.

anything from a lute to a cittern or the bass-toned bandora (stringed instruments and the sixteenth-century forerunners of the modern acoustic guitar). There would have been trumpets, flutes, organs, harpsichords and other piano-like devices such as the popular virginal or spinet.

But music was not performed purely for a seated audience. What is a feast without dancing? You could show off your finery and your agility as the musicians struck up and you joined a partner to leap and stamp, spin and jump and hop in the latest athletic galliard, a fast-moving and exciting dance that swept across Europe during the sixteenth century. Statelier was the measured pavane, a slow processional form of dance where couples moved together, the lady resting her hand on that of her partner. The steps were long and gliding with flourishes in the form of curtsies and back steps.

Dancing at court was generally between couples, a man and a woman. It was perfectly in order for the female partner to ask the gentleman to take the floor with her. To refuse an invitation to stand up and dance was considered ill mannered.

One dance did cause some raised eyebrows. The daring la volta (or lavolta), a particularly vigorous version of the galliard, required some close contact and fast lifting and turning, where the gentleman had to place his hand beneath a lady's bottom to lift her high in the air.

Even more entertaining was the prospect of a masque – almost a masked ball with music. Actors set the scene by the light of flaring torches while the guests, wearing fancy dress and their features disguised by elaborate masks, paraded. Then the dancing and feasting began before the dramatic moment at the end when masks were whipped away and partners discovered each other. Henry VIII had a band of 'interlude players', who were actors hired to give entertainment, and he loved masques or 'dysguisings'. It was at Greenwich Palace in 1513 that he gave the first masquerade as a Christmas entertainment.

Men and women danced together in taverns, where musicians played, using their huge repertoire of folk and country dances. As the evening progressed, partners

Rustic pleasures such as country dancing were widespread in Tudor England. (With kind permission of the Thomas Fisher Rare Book Library, University of Toronto)

In 1508 Prince Henry (later Henry VIII) competed in the summer jousting tournaments at Greenwich and Richmond for the first time. It became obvious to all who watched this tall (Henry stood at 6ft 2in), slim, athletic, fiery-haired youngster 'running at the ring' – charging on horseback towards a small hanging hoop, his lance aloft, lowering his weapon at the last possible moment to spear the hoop with perfect precision – that he was a skilled and brilliant performer. But Henry, chafing at the bit, had to take a back seat while others indulged in personal armed combat. His life, as heir to the throne, was too precious.

were swapped in musical progression and everyone had the chance to hold hands and move to a simple sequence of steps.

Morris dancing – yet another form of entertainment set to music – survives today in the twenty-first century. One of the earliest written records mentioning this dance is of a payment of 7s by the Goldsmith's Company in 1448 to a morris troop. By the time Henry VII became king in 1485, the custom of morris dancing, with a set of jingling bells strapped on to every performer's shins, handkerchiefs on their wrists, and swords and sticks to wave in time to the music, was well established. It is thought the name comes from a Moorish dance, but whatever the origins, morris dancing became a firm part of traditional English entertainment, especially at Whitsun, when troupes would be paid to perform for landowners anxious to entertain their holiday house parties.

The many forms of entertainment we take for granted now – cards, dice, bowls, tennis, even football and others that we are not so familiar with, such as shovegroat (an early form of shoveha'penny), quoits and ninepins

The Tudor love of seeing animals suffer, as they delighted in cruel sports such as bear-baiting, cockfighting (or cocking) and bull-baiting, is alien to most of us today. All classes and both sexes loved to spend their Sundays at the cockpits, where bets were placed and much money changed hands. A good fighting cock would cost the enormous sum of £5. Henry VIII loved the sport, building a cockpit next to the Palace of Whitehall. Bear-baiting, where a tethered bear was set upon by mastiffs until all the beasts were covered with blood and saliva and the bear was overcome, happened most days, as did bull-baiting.

– were expressly forbidden. This was not a deliberate act of repression but an attempt to force every Englishman to practise his archery. This had been so since medieval times and Henry VIII reinforced the law in 1542, so that there should be a skilled force of archers to draw on.

If you were a nobleman, a knight or a member of the gentry with more than £100 a year to your name, you could indulge in a game of backgammon, a round of shovegroat or dice. The rest of society was required to keep a bow and four arrows at all times and to practise shooting on every 'holy day' or holiday; sons were to be trained to shoot and woe betide anyone discovered playing bowls or dice instead.

❀ SPORTING LIFE ❀

Hunting and fishing were other hugely popular pastimes for the wealthier classes to enjoy and here sex was no bar. If you could stay with the chase, twisting and turning, galloping across pasture and weaving through woodland in pursuit of a great red deer stag, it did not matter whether you were male or female. Queen Elizabeth, an energetic horsewoman, loved to hunt, as did many Tudor noblewomen.

Hawking, too, a popular royal sport, was theirs to enjoy.

Wrestling was strictly a male-only sport, although many Tudor women must have enjoyed the spectacle of the local males stripping down to their breeches and tussling mightily until one threw the other to the ground and held him fast there. On feast days and market days strong young men competed with each other to win the prize ram.

But the game of football, played by working men on Sundays, was a murderous one. Teams could include as many players as they wished and the 'pitch' could be whatever size the teams chose – a couple of city streets or a few fields between two villages. The ball, of heavy leather, could be picked up, as in modern rugby, and anyone from the opposing team could be tripped, punched, kicked or otherwise impeded. It was not uncommon for an inquest to be held after a game; the verdict was usually 'manslaughter'.

❀ THE PLAY'S THE THING ❀

The form of entertainment that saw the greatest advance over the Tudor period, and which was enjoyed across the class divide and by men and women alike, was the theatre. When Henry VII took the throne in 1485, medieval mystery plays and miracle plays were standard fare up and down the country and the same plays were performed by regular troupes year after year. But as Catholicism went out of favour, so did these plays, the Privy Council decreeing that they should not be performed. But new works began to appear. Plays telling stories of love, morality and history were written and staged. Companies of actors,

Elizabeth I, depicted here on her royal seal, was a great supporter of the arts, and had her own theatre company, the Queen's Men. (THP)

each attached to a nobleman – Lord Strange's Men, Lord Leicester's Men, the Lord Admiral's Men – began to perform across the length and breadth of the country. As this form of theatre became increasingly popular, London was a magnet for the art and shows were put on in galleried inns and other public spaces.

During Queen Elizabeth's reign, theatres were built, despite opposition from the Puritans who saw this new form of entertainment as blasphemous and sinful. John Brayne and John Burbage built The Theatre at Shoreditch, which was joined soon after by The Curtain. The Swan and The Rose followed hard on their heels. Elizabeth gave her seal of approval, establishing her own company of actors, the Queen's Men. Thomas Kyd and Christopher Marlowe began to put on their great plays, *The Spanish Tragedy* and *Tamburlaine the Great*, while a consortium of actors, writers and impresarios, including William Shakespeare, and Cuthbert and Richard Burbage built a magnificent theatre at Southwark in 1599. It was called The Globe.

The three great playwrights of this richly flourishing era were Shakespeare, Marlowe and Ben Jonson. The large

London audiences had plenty of choice with around thirty plays being performed in each of the theatres annually. Queues snaked round the streets outside as theatregoers waited for entrance (standing room only), which cost 1*d*. Galleried spaces where you would still stand, but were under cover, set customers back 2*d*, as did a space upstairs. The rich could hire a box for 6*d*.

3

IN SICKNESS
AND IN HEALTH

ing Henry VII and his queen were asleep in
their beds at Greenwich Palace when a sealed
letter arrived from the court of their son,
Arthur, Prince of Wales. Trusted messengers
had travelled for two days from Ludlow
Castle in the Welsh Marches to bring the terrible news that
the young prince, heir to the throne and newly married to
Catherine of Aragon, was dead.

It is not certain what sudden illness killed the 15-year-
old Prince Arthur on 2 April 1502, but it is likely to have
been the dreaded sweating sickness, a flu-like affliction that
was swift and deadly. Just as the plague was feared, so was
this illness which suddenly appeared in England in 1485,
returning in waves until 1556 when it seemed to disappear.
The terrible nature of the disease, whose victims suffered a
raging temperature, convulsions and unbearable stomach
cramps, was that it struck suddenly and killed often within
hours of the first symptoms.

In the hot summer of 1508 the sweating sickness swept
through London again. Contemporary accounts write
of citizens enjoying their main meal at 11 a.m., feeling
perfectly healthy as they ate and lying dead by suppertime.
King Henry VII began to panic as the disease infected and
killed members of his staff. The complete royal household

Medice, cura te ipsum . *Luc: 4.*

The doctor carried off by death. (With kind permission of the Thomas Fisher Rare Book Library, University of Toronto)

upped sticks and moved from the pestilence that seemed to have invaded the whole of London. From the hoped-for safety of his manor house, Wanstead Hall, in Essex, he issued an edict that no-one from London should be allowed on the estate and that no-one from his household was to travel back to the city for any reason, unless they were physicians or apothecaries.

Over the decades, tens of thousands died from the sweating sickness, including, in 1528, Elizabeth Wyckes, the wife of Thomas Cromwell, later Chief Minister to

The French ambassador to the English court, Du Bellai, noted in May 1528 that one of Mademoiselle Boleyn's ladies-in-waiting had been stricken by the sweating sickness. 'The King left in great haste, and went a dozen miles off,' he wrote:

> This disease is the easiest in the world to die of. You have a slight pain in the head and at the heart; all at once you begin to sweat. There is no need for a physician: for if you uncover yourself the least in the world, or cover yourself a little too much, you are taken off without languishing. It is true that if you merely put your hand out of bed during the first 24 hours ... you become stiff.

King Henry VIII. Their two daughters, Grace and Anne, both died of the same disease a year after their mother.

Henry VIII, like his father, was terrified of contracting this lethal disease; if it struck anyone at court, he would hastily leave for another of his palaces or great houses. He is said to have spent much time studying remedies for the illness, from herbs laced with molasses to the efficacy of bleeding various parts of the body.

❋ A DREADED PLAGUE ❋

Life expectancy for Tudor men and women was low – around 41 years of age in the 1580s. In country areas, more than 20 per cent of children died before their tenth birthday and that figure was higher in towns and cities where disease was more prevalent.

Poor hygiene, polluted water, shortage of food and disease made early death commonplace in rich and poor households alike, although the rich did have the advantage of being able to afford food, the means to keep warm in winter and the opportunity to keep themselves and their houses clean.

Portrait of Elizabeth I from her prayer book, printed in 1578. Prayer was relied upon, in an era when science and medicine were baffled by outbreaks of plague and other maladies, as a guard against sickness and disease. (THP)

Probably the most effective measure against the plague, from 1578 onwards, was the most horrible. Thick boards were nailed firmly across doors and windows of the homes of victims where the afflicted person and his or her whole family, servants included, were isolated inside for at least six weeks. Watchmen kept guard to ensure that no-one left the house.

But commonly occurring diseases, such as influenza and malaria and, worst of all, the 'pestilence' or plague, struck without respecting the status of the victim. During the fifteenth, sixteenth and seventeenth centuries there was little that could be done to avoid these illnesses, especially the dreaded plague.

The plague – symptoms of which included painful black 'buboes', or swellings, of the lymph nodes that occurred in the neck, groin and armpits of victims – was, it is thought, carried by rat fleas. It first appeared in England in 1348 and thence intermittently over the next 300 years or so. Its cause was not known in those days, when fleas and rats were regarded as a nuisance but an unavoidable part of life. Infection was worse in the summer, when rats and their fleas were more prevalent, and the rich were better able to escape, simply by packing up and moving to the country or to households where there was no sign of the disease.

Physicians prescribed mithridate, an antidote to poison made up of dozens of ingredients, but it was probably no use at all. Perfuming the sickroom or burning a blazing fire therein did not help either. Sometimes the pustules were burst, using a young pigeon's feather, but this probably helped to spread the infection rather than do any good. By 1578, during Elizabeth's reign, parliament got a grip and made a list of measures to limit the outbreaks.

There were to be inspections reviewing the causes of death where plague was suspected and magistrates were to be informed so that the progress of the disease could be charted. All the clothing and bedding of victims was to be piled on to bonfires.

❧ POXES AND THE FLUX ❧

If the plague didn't strike, there was always the danger of the 'bloody flux' – a nasty dysentery which was caused by poor sanitation and infected food – or typhus, spread by lice, or typhoid fever. Also common were the two poxes: smallpox and the great pox, or syphilis, also known as the 'French disease', which affected all classes. One of the recommended cures for this disease was to sweat it out in an early form of sauna that was liberally strewn with herbs and then to rub scented oil over the body.

It might seem strange that mosquito-carried malaria was common in Tudor England, where it was referred to as 'the ague'. However, because the mosquitoes bred rapidly on low-lying marshy ground, this was where it struck. People living on or near the Norfolk Broads and the Wash, the Fens in Cambridge and Lincolnshire, and Romney Marsh were greatly afflicted and thousands died. The name 'malaria' was coined to describe the 'bad air' that rose, miasma-like, from the thick wet ground. It was this, the Tudors thought, that brought the disease, which killed rich and poor alike. It did not occur to them that the malaria was carried by biting insects.

Smallpox was no respecter of persons either. The queen herself, Elizabeth I, was laid low by a bad attack in October 1562. She took to the royal bedchamber but, despite all expectations, survived the unpleasant illness, which came with a high temperature and aching muscles, vomiting and diarrhoea, and an eruption of small pus-filled blisters over the face and body. As her illness worsened, the question of succession was uppermost in the minds of her ministers, who held several meetings to decide the issue should she succumb.

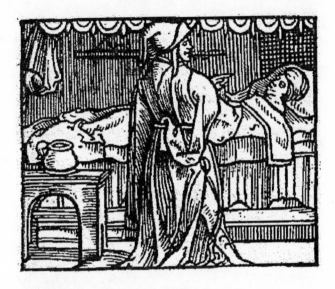

Pox victim receiving treatment. (Library of Congress, LC-USZ62-95250)

She was at Hampton Court when she fell ill and, because of the highly contagious nature of the disease, there were few volunteers from the ranks of her ladies-in-waiting to nurse her. Loyal Lady Mary Sidney stayed by Elizabeth's side, bathing the queen and changing her linen until, miraculously, she recovered. Poor Lady Mary also contracted the disease, recovering, but becoming horribly disfigured by the scars left on her face. It is not recorded who cared for her.

❁ DENTAL WOES ❁

There were plenty of recipes for breath-fresheners in this era as bad breath was endemic, the product of horribly rotten teeth and decaying food caught between them. Most people had gaps where teeth had been pulled or had fallen out, and a mouth full of discoloured and rotting teeth was not uncommon – Queen Elizabeth's teeth were completely black by the time she reached old age. The use of toothpicks to remove scraps of food was common practice, as was a piece of damp linen (a tooth-cloth) sprinkled with alum and used daily to scrub the teeth. Powdered cuttlefish, salt, soot and chalk were all recommended as tooth powders, which were rubbed on before being rinsed away with a mixture of white wine and sulphuric acid. It is said that Queen Elizabeth and

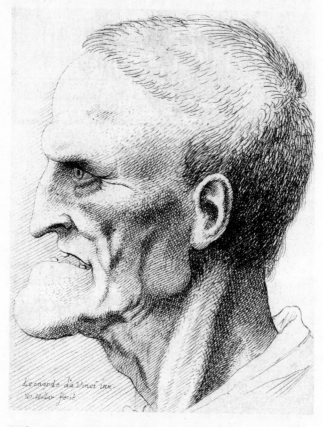

Bad teeth were an everyday – and painful – feature of Tudor life. (With kind permission of the Thomas Fisher Rare Book Library, University of Toronto)

other high-born ladies would stuff perfumed handkerchiefs in their mouth to take away the taint of foul breath.

Much more pleasant were the recipes for rosemary flowers steeped in water and used as a mouthwash, while cloves were also used for this purpose and tucked into the side of the mouth to keep breath sweet.

Furry tongues would be scrubbed or scraped, while spicy seeds such as cumin or aniseed could be chewed to disguise bad breath.

In the days before effective painkillers, another dreaded affliction was toothache. When the pain became unbearable, the only course of action was to take the offending molar out. A blacksmith would not charge too much to wrench it with his pliers but there were more expensive specialist teeth drawers who used 'pelicans' – bone-handled levers with hooks shaped like a pelican's bill – to ease the aching tooth out.

Tudor physicians believed that the four humours ruled your health and your disposition.

Choler or yellow bile, black bile, phlegm and blood should be in balance, they thought, or things would go awry and illness would follow. These humours corresponded with basic elements: earth, air, fire and water, which in turn were linked to parts of the body. Medical opinion of the day held that this balance could be affected by foul air, or miasmas, rising from stagnant water, bogs or swamps, or from eating fish or fruit or even unrefined brown bread. Witchcraft could be a factor, too, as could the Lord striking someone down with illness or disease, so that they and their friends and family would understand the virtue of suffering. No wonder the apothecaries issued not only medicines such as wormwood, galingale and cassia, but also small cards printed with prayers.

⚫ CLOSE-STOOLS AND CHAMBER POTS ⚫

Like it or not – and most didn't – there was no getting away from the stench that arose from Tudor privies. Countrymen and women had gardens in which they could conceal their 'place of easement' but it was more difficult for those living in a crowded town.

Tudors were less coy than people today about relieving themselves in public places and quite often at dinners and banquets, the rushes, strewn on the floor, served to mop up more than spilt gravy.

Chamber pots were generally used at night time and the waste emptied into a public cesspit or a water-filled gully flowing down the middle of the street. Irresponsible citizens were known to fling the contents of their pots from upper-storey windows – yet another hazard for urban Tudors – although if the offending tippers were caught, they could be fined. It is recorded that travellers staying away from home often defecated or urinated in fireplaces or in a corner of the room if no chamber pot was provided. Some privies were set above cesspits, connected to them by a stone chimney which stank because of the filth that had accumulated and stuck to the bricks and stonework over the years.

The courtier in the king's privy chamber known as the Groom of the Stool was closer than any other to the monarch. Henry VII's Groom of the Stool, Hugh Denys, was the man selected to provide the king's commode and the necessary washing equipment. It is probable that he actually washed Henry after the king had used the commode or 'close-stool'. Denys became a powerful man – he controlled access to Henry and was responsible for providing the king's day-to-day necessities – eventually becoming his private treasurer, setting up an account that became known as the privy purse.

Queen Elizabeth followed the example of her godson, Sir John Harington, who had a flushing lavatory built at his house near Bath. She had a similar contraption at Richmond. Her father, Henry VIII, used a 'chair of easement' embellished with a gold-studded padded seat. His servants shared a very public lavatory, a twenty-eight-seater built so that it hung strategically over the waters of the River Thames.

Richer town dwellers had a commode-like seat known as a 'close-stool', often elaborately upholstered to resemble a plush chair. The centre was cut away and a pot fitted beneath. Disposal of the contents was done by the servants.

Mansions and castles still used the medieval 'garderobes' – rooms so called because, along with the 'seat of easement', they also served as wardrobes for clothes and valuables. The seat itself, of wood or stone with a hole in the centre, would be set into a tiny room which jutted out of an exterior wall high above a moat, river or purpose-built cesspit. A chute sped the noisome contents on their way to the water or dung-heap below, which was periodically cleared away by some unfortunate servant.

The wealthy wiped and cleaned themselves with a damp linen cloth or piece of soft lamb's wool which would be washed (not by them) and used again, while the poor made do with a chunk of damp moss or some leaves.

❀ A LONG HOT SOAK? ❀

Personal hygiene was a lot easier for the rich than for the poor. Bathing was not a regular occupation; in fact, more than two or three times a year was considered detrimental to health. Filling a wooden bath with hot water and emptying it afterwards was a lengthy task for the servants, who would also often line the bath with fine linen cloths to prevent splinters from the wood injuring their master or mistress. Imported perfumed oils would be added to the hot water and soap, made from scented olive oil, was used. Sponge baths – pewter bowls full of heated water, carried to bedrooms by servants – were probably more usual than complete immersion in a steaming bath tub, while many, conscious of the need to smell sweet and fragrant, would rub their bodies with perfumed oils to take away and cover natural, if unpleasant, odours.

By the latter part of Elizabeth's reign, the very rich would have installed one of the newfangled boiler rooms, with a stove and two tanks of water, each filled by servants. The stove would heat one of these tanks while pipes from each fed the hot and cold water through a wall into the bathing room, where crude taps allowed it to be poured into a conveniently placed tub. Emptying the water was yet another job for the servants. King Henry VIII had such a bathroom built into his private suite in the Bayne Tower at Hampton Court in 1529. The apartment already housed an office and study, library and jewel house, and Henry's bedroom. The new bathroom, with its elaborate gold and white ceiling, backed on to a small boiler room which housed a charcoal-fired stove for heating the water which was drawn, via a system known as the Coombe Conduit, from nearby springs.

Tudors had ambivalent feelings about water. They believed that any infection it carried would be absorbed into their bodies if they relaxed in a deep bath. So bathing was only undertaken when the source of the water was known to be pure, such as a well or a spring. River water was 'troubled' – that is, polluted. The fear that infections from water could be absorbed through the pores may have come from the days of the fifteenth-century bathing houses that sprang up around London where female attendants helped men and women wash in hot tubs. The men were often helped to more than a mere wash, so that syphilis became rife. Those who became infected at the baths blamed the suspicious properties of hot water.

In addition to a loo that flushed, Queen Elizabeth seemed to enjoy bathing, taking a portable bath with her when she travelled. In her palace at Whitehall was a bathing arrangement with water flowing from shells, while her Windsor Palace bathroom had large mirrors covering the walls. A much-quoted letter, written by the Venetian ambassador at the time, reported that the queen bathed at least monthly, 'whether she needs it or not'. At a period in the past when baths were considered a necessity only at times of sickness, the queen was clearly fastidious about personal hygiene, bathing regularly. When not bathing she would be washed by her ladies, who filled pewter bowls with warm water, using linen cloths to clean her skin. Her teeth were scrubbed with cloths soaked in a mixture of vinegar, honey and white wine.

✿ USEFUL INSTRUMENTS ✿

Inside a Tudor 'make-up bag' or 'wash bag' could be found small mirrors made of steel or glass and useful implements such as the double-ended bone instrument with tweezers at one end and a tiny scoop for cleaning the ears at the other. Very little mention is made in contemporary documents about how women coped with their menstrual flow, but household accounts show unexplained quantities of fine linen and ribbon, leaving historians to assume that these were to be made into sanitary towels and belts, or even rolled into tampons.

Linen in large quantities was another useful tool in the constant battle against smelliness. Linen towels would be used (by the richer classes) for rubbing the body all over to wipe off the sweat and dirt, while they would don fine woollen or linen shifts, or undergarments, changing them frequently, possibly daily, to absorb all unpleasant body smells, leaving the outerwear reasonably clean and fragrant. The family linen – towels, shirts, shifts and hose – would be laundered carefully to ensure that everyone stayed sweet-smelling.

Alas for the very poor, who had few garments and very little chance of washing them: there was small hope of being anything other than smelly. There was also every likelihood that parasites, such as lice and fleas, which carried the major diseases of the time, would hop aboard and live comfortably on the sufferer's skin without danger of being dislodged.

🏵 Home-Grown Remedies 🏵

Medical assistance, in the shape of doctors or apothecaries, was expensive, so the first to be called on when illness struck were the women in the community, who would pool their knowledge to ease pains and to aid the suffering.

At the beginning of the sixteenth century, not many women were able to read or write, but by 1600 at least 10 per cent could do both. It was for these women that the Tudor equivalent of modern self-help manuals were written and published in English, guiding housewives in the brewing of remedies and mixing of poultices and compounds in order to ease complaints ranging from common colds to broken bones.

Some of these remedies were not unpleasant and had foundation in the true healing properties of herbs and plants. For example, comfrey was known in Tudor times as 'knitbone' and modern research shows that the plant does indeed have medicinal qualities. Broken bones would be manipulated back into position and a poultice of pounded comfrey leaves wrapped around the area to aid the mending or 'knitting' of the bone. Minor wounds, torn ligaments or aching joints would be treated with a sweet-smelling ointment made with olive oil or sweet almond oil, young comfrey leaves and beeswax, cooked slowly together before being allowed to cool and solidify.

But some sixteenth-century recipes to aid recovery sound worse than the illness. A 1585 book recommends that 'broken sinews' should be healed with a poultice of finely crushed young worms, while another book advises that toothache should be cured with the swilling round the mouth of a brew of henbane (which is extremely poisonous) soaked in vinegar and rosewater. Body lice were prevalent and there were many remedies suggested for getting rid of these unpleasant parasites. One involved sticking mercury to a wide linen belt using solid grease then tying it around the afflicted person, while another suggests that ground-up frankincense, stirred into boar's fat and rubbed in well, would do the trick.

Those bothered by sores and ulcers could be given an ointment, made at home, that consisted of seaweed, olive oil, turpentine, bugloss juice, parsley juice and rosin (a form of resin obtained from pine trees) cooked with fat from deer or sheep, which was strained and solidified.

Insomniacs were advised to try a potion made with a spoonful of rosewater, the same amount of 'woman's milk' and lettuce juice boiled up together. It was not to be taken by mouth, but used to soak a wide linen cloth to be bound around the head after being sprinkled with grated nutmeg.

There were many recipes for soups to aid recovery in non-specified illnesses. They include a broth made from ground almonds and cream, the brain of a chicken and sugar. Much nicer sounding were the ever-popular 'caudles'. These were nourishing drinks, often made especially for the very old and young. An old man in need of a quick pick-me-up might be given a caudle made with a pint of muscadine (a sweet wine) mixed with some ale, egg yolks, sugar and mace or nutmeg, heated gently until it thickened and served in a bowl with chunks of bread broken into it, to give it some substance.

A basic caudle could be made with some white wine mixed with almond milk and heated slowly with sugar and strained egg yolks until nice and thick. Sometimes it might be decorated with a sprinkling of alkenade (a red powder made from the ground-up root of alkanet, a plant in the borage family) or yellow saffron and nutmeg.

❁ SEND FOR THE DOCTOR ❁

If all else failed, sick Tudors would send to town for the help of a physician, who was responsible for identifying and treating illnesses, a surgeon who dealt with broken bones and anything occurring on the surface of the body, such as wounds and sores, or an apothecary, who would mix and dispense the remedies ordered by the physician or surgeon. It might be that the illness was an obvious one, in which case the apothecary would be the first port of call for a simple remedy.

It was really a case of paying your money (the considerable sum of 13s for a physician's treatment of a wealthy patient undergoing a serious illness) and taking your chances. Throughout the early Tudor period there were very few fully qualified medical practitioners, although by the end of Elizabeth's reign in 1603 there were more than 2,000 operating throughout the country.

Although medical knowledge was growing slowly, the belief that the influence of the four humours and the basic elements of air, earth, fire and water still ruled the health of everyone was widely held. Blood-letting – opening a vein and taking out a small quantity of blood – was done routinely, to bring those vital humours back into balance. Most sixteenth-century physicians also believed in the influence of the stars, so they would automatically

Most Tudor households would wash and clean bedclothes regularly, in an effort to get rid of any fleas or lice inhabiting the sheets and blankets. They would also ensure that plates, bowls and cooking pots were scrubbed and cleaned after each meal with plenty of hot water and would use straw and potash to scour away any pieces of meat or fish that might have stuck fast. When they were thoroughly clean, they would be left to drain on the scullery board. Drinking flasks, spoons and other cutlery were given a similar treatment, but the diners would have their own knives, kept in leather sheaths on their belts, which they wiped carefully after use.

calculate their position and the planets in the night sky at the time the illness set in. The doctors of the sixteenth century were also very keen on diagnosis based on the colour, smell, consistency and even taste of a patient's urine. If it was a deep ruddy colour or dark gold it was likely, said one expert, that the illness was based in the liver and the stomach. If, however, it was thin, it was probable that the body contained too much phlegm, thus encouraging fever of some sort. And so on.

Many herbal remedies were used but there were some outlandish prescriptions on record, including a dose of powdered Egyptian mummy, while tobacco, arsenic, dried toad and lily root were all employed at one time or another.

Surgeons had to have a strong stomach and knew they must act quickly when people were injured, especially on the battlefield, when wounds needed to be sewn up, bones set and limbs amputated. If a surgeon moved fast after the accident, the body's own defences acted as natural painkillers as the offending limb was sawn away. When the pain became too great, opiates and alcohol were given. But the main cause of death after surgery was infection,

Early surgery was fraught with perils. (THP)

something that was not taken into consideration or understood, as the operation went ahead. Instruments were wiped and washed, but the process of sterilisation was never considered and lethal blood poisoning was common, killing many thousands of people.

4

FRIENDS
AND FOES

he Lancastrian Henry Tudor's claim to the throne was not rock solid – and he knew it. One of his first acts, when parliament was convened in November 1485, just a month after his coronation, was to backdate the start of his reign to the day before the Battle of Bosworth, when he had defeated the Yorkist king, Richard III. In doing so, he rewrote history to make himself the legitimate king and Richard the usurper. Therefore, in theory, all those who had supported Richard were traitors.

Although Henry pardoned former enemies who swore to support him and very soon married Elizabeth, the daughter of the Yorkist Edward IV, to unite the warring houses of York and Lancaster, not everyone was content to see him rule. The first years of his reign were tense with fear and suspicion as conspiracies and treachery threatened to see the Tudor dynasty fall and die.

His wife Elizabeth of York's young brothers, Edward and Richard, would have inherited the throne in turn had not their uncle, Richard III, removed them from the scene. Another strong claimant was the 12-year-old Edward, Earl of Warwick, another nephew of Edward IV, but Henry had already dealt with that one, imprisoning the boy in the Tower.

🏵 A YOUNG PRETENDER 🏵

So when, on Whit Sunday 24 May 1487, a young boy, calling himself the Earl of Warwick and claiming to have escaped from imprisonment in the Tower of London, was paraded in front of a Yorkist crowd in Ireland before being crowned 'King of England' in Christ Church Cathedral, Dublin, Henry mustered his troops and made ready for battle.

The mastermind behind this particular plot was another Yorkist: the Plantagenet John de la Pole, Earl of Lincoln, who, with his aunt, Margaret of York, planned the whole deception. Henry was ready for them. Lincoln's army, headed by the young pretender, crossed the Irish Sea, landing in Cumberland, and marched south to meet the king's forces. The clash came at East Stoke, a village in Nottinghamshire. It was no contest. Lincoln (who, as nephew to Richard III and Edward IV, also had a reasonable claim to the throne in his own right) was slaughtered, and his troops routed and massacred. The fake Earl of Warwick was found, alive. Henry paraded the real one, a simple-minded boy fresh from his incarceration in the Tower, through the streets of London to show his people the difference, before sending him back to prison.

The boy groomed by Lincoln to impersonate the young Earl of Warwick was known as Lambert Simnel, the son of an Oxford tradesman. Lambert may not have been his real name. He had been given some polish early on by a priest after spotting potential in the boy, who was only about 10 or 11 at the time of the uprising. Henry, realising that the lad was a mere figurehead in Lincoln's plot, pardoned him, setting him to work in the royal kitchens. He is said to have become a skilful falconer in later life.

🏵 AND ANOTHER ONE ... 🏵

One pretender to the throne is bad enough, but poor Henry was faced with another, much more serious threat in the shape of a personable young man claiming to be not a nephew of the dead Plantagenet Edward IV, but his younger son, Richard, Duke of York. It was the disappearance into the Tower of London of Richard and his older brother Edward that had, in part, legitimised Henry Tudor's own claim to the throne. Perkin Warbeck, the son of a Flemish man from Tournai, was discovered by Yorkist malcontents in the Irish port of Cork, where the ship on which he was serving had docked. He was 16, blonde, good looking and fond of expensive clothes. Warbeck was groomed for the throne and disappeared across the water to France. But after a half-hearted invasion of France by Henry, a peace treaty between the two countries made Warbeck fear extradition to England, so he fled to Belgium, where he was taken in by Margaret of Burgundy, Edward IV's sister. She claimed that he was certainly her nephew, the missing Richard, and he found support from her and other European courts who refused to extradite Warbeck to England, despite Henry's requests.

By 1493, news that the young Prince Richard (aka Perkin Warbeck) was alive, well and ready to claim his throne spread like wildfire around Europe and back to England. Henry was outraged and retaliated by imposing trade sanctions. The Habsburg king, Maximilian, in support of Warbeck, hit back with his own embargoes. Discontent, both political and economic, threatened in England and abroad. Rumour abounded and everywhere the Tudor king's spies heard of plots to assassinate Henry, including one that involved painting surfaces in the royal palace with a deadly poison. Then, in 1494, at the funeral in Vienna of Maximilian's father Frederick, the Holy Roman Emperor, Warbeck was shown off as the 'King of England', and paraded through the Netherlands and Belgium as such.

The following year, with the backing of Maximilian, he led an invasion, landing at Deal in Kent. But Henry had got wind of the plot and his soldiers massacred the advance party, while Warbeck himself, still on board the ship, evaded capture. Then he turned up in Scotland, married the beautiful Katherine Gordon and was again proclaimed 'King of England', this time by James IV.

🌹 Not One Rebellion, but Two 🌹

Henry demanded that parliament grant him the power to tax heavily to pay for military action – and this triggered another rebellion, more terrifying than that engendered by Warbeck's supporters. In 1497, just as Henry's forces were moving north to root out Warbeck and his men, thousands of Cornishmen, outraged by the punitive taxation, marched on London. The city was besieged as the rebels camped at Blackheath, ready for the confrontation. The queen, the king's mother and royal children were taken to the Tower for safety. The royal troops were recalled from their long march north as the Cornishmen

The Tower of London, where the Royal Family took refuge. (With kind permission of the Thomas Fisher Rare Book Library, University of Toronto)

Henry Tudor left no stone unturned in his quest to discover the double agents and traitors in his camp. His spies were everywhere; in the homes of suspects, always interviewing and questioning. He found that two men holding high office in his own household were working closely with the conspirators. The first was his Lord Steward Lord John Fitzwalter, the man in charge of the royal household 'below stairs'. More disconcertingly, the second was his own step-uncle, his Lord Chamberlain, Sir William Stanley. Sir William had control over court entertainment, the movements of the royal household and entry to the king's presence. Both men were tried and executed. When Stanley's house was searched, Henry's men discovered Yorkist emblems and £10,000 in cash; the king suspected it was intended to pay for an army.

were subdued, their leaders hanged, drawn and quartered and their tarred heads stuck on spikes on London Bridge as a grim reminder to anyone who might be thinking rebellious thoughts.

Warbeck, meanwhile, thinking to take advantage of the Cornish rebellion, sailed from Scotland to land at Whitesand Bay in the south-west, but by the time he reached Taunton the game was up and he fled to seek sanctuary at Beaulieu Abbey in Hampshire. But Henry winkled him out of there and took him to London, where he was made a figure of fun and ridicule. For two years Warbeck was looked after by guards, but by 1499 he and the real Earl of Warwick, still incarcerated in the Tower, were the focus of those still wanting to oust the king. Eventually both were tried and condemned. Warbeck died by the hangman's noose at Tyburn and Warwick by the executioner's axe on Tower Green.

Henry VII, the first of five Tudor monarchs – three of them the children of Henry VIII by three different mothers – died unmourned by many. Towards the end of his life his need to collect taxes by fines, dues, penalties and confiscations had become an obsession. His tax collectors devised ever more cunning ways of screwing money out of his people, from the nobility to newly rich merchants, making him ever more unpopular and feared. All these collections were overseen by the king, who checked each page of the account books with care before scrawling a huge 'H' on each page. Yet for all his eagerness to fill the treasury, he was surprisingly generous with small gifts of money. In 1493, for instance, his privy purse accounts show that, in January, he paid the choristers at 'Paul's and St Stephen, 13s 4d' and gave the princely sum of £1 to an unnamed musician 'for making of a song'. In May the 'Padesey piper on the bagpipe' was given 6s 8d and in August the huge amount of £30 went to 'the young damsel that danceth'.

ANOTHER KING, DIFFERENT ENEMIES

Because of his father's unpopularity and his own attractive looks and personality, the accession of the 17-year-old Henry VIII was greeted with joy, which seemed to flow throughout England. He was good looking, spoke several languages and accomplished in the courtly arts of musical composition and singing. He wrote well and excelled at sport from jousting, horsemanship and hunting to tennis, javelin throwing, archery and bowls. He also had the advantage of taking over a country with a bulging treasury and a settled system of administration.

But he was his father's son, quick and ruthless to take advantage. The men about him, jostling for position and favour, and eager to disassociate themselves with any part they might have played in his father's repressive regime, knew that scapegoats must be found and punishment applied. Senior councillors pointed the finger at lawyers Richard Empson and Edmund Dudley, ministers and members of the old king's council, who had been at the

One of the strangest episodes in Henry VIII's reign was his preoccupation with Elizabeth Barton, the so-called 'Holy Nun of Kent' or the 'Mad Maid of Kent', depending on your point of view of her 'prophesies'. When she was around 20 years old, Barton, a poor woman from the serving classes, began to have prophetic visions which seemed to come true. Her visions, upholding the Catholic faith, encouraging pilgrimages and praying to the Virgin Mary, became increasingly religious and, at the time, were in tune with Henry's own views as a staunch supporter of the pope. But when Henry, in his bid to divorce Catherine, set in train the English Reformation and sought to take control of the Church himself, her prophesies were directed at him. In 1532 Barton, by then a nun at the Benedictine order of St Sepulchre in Canterbury, foretold that if he went ahead and remarried, he would die within the year and go to hell. She even described the place in hell set aside for the king. In 1533 she was arrested and forced to confess that her prophecies were fabricated. Poor Elizabeth was hanged for treason at Tyburn, and buried at Greyfriars church in Newgate Street but without her head. She won the dubious distinction of becoming the only woman ever to have had her head displayed on a spike on London Bridge.

forefront of extracting money from thousands of people. On the day that Henry's death was announced (three days after he actually died on 21 April 1509) there were dawn raids on the houses of both men. They were thrown in the Tower, accused of treason. On 18 August 1510 they were brought to Tower Hill to face the jeering of the crowds before they were beheaded on the public scaffold.

Like his father before him, Henry VIII would do everything in his power to achieve his goals; both believed unwaveringly in the supremacy of kingship. Henry Tudor was ruthless in the use of taxation and imprisonment to fill his coffers; his son would later do anything within his means in order to rid himself of wives who did not give him a male heir. If that meant using the executioner's sword, so be it.

And Henry VIII regarded as foes anyone who might present a threat to his Crown. In the early part of his reign he had Edmund de la Pole, Earl of Suffolk, a Yorkist with a legitimate claim to the throne, beheaded, even though the man had been incarcerated in the Tower for years. The same fate befell Edward Stafford, Duke of Buckingham, who was a direct descendant of the Plantagenet Edward III.

FIGHTING FOR THE POPE

Henry was a true believer and a great champion of the papacy – for the first two decades of his reign. His lust for glory, war and power, and the vision of himself as a reborn Henry V or King Arthur fighting just wars, took him into a 'holy war' against France in 1513, a couple of years after he had joined the Holy League to defend the papacy. Louis XII of France was threatening to depose the pope and Henry was determined to prevent him and cover himself in glory at the same time. Cardinal Wolsey, the great organiser of both Church and State in England during the early part of Henry's reign, saw to it that parliament voted for a decent amount of war taxation and the best-equipped English

Contemporary engraving of the Battle of the Spurs. (THP)

army since the Battle of Agincourt. Henry led his troops, defeating the French at the Battle of Guinegate (now known as Enguinegatte) in Pas-de-Calais. The encounter became known as the Battle of the Spurs because of the indecent haste with which the French cavalry left the field. Henry also took the towns of Thérouranne and Tournai, then arrived home covered in glory and gleeful because his friend, the pope, stripped the French king of his title 'Most Christian King' and awarded it to Henry.

During his absence in France, another foe had a go at Henry and England. His own brother-in-law, James IV of Scotland (who was married to Henry's sister, Margaret), urged on by his French allies, invaded England. But the troops back home, overseen by Henry's queen, Catherine, routed the Scots at Branxton near Flodden in Northumbria, killing James and at least 12,000 Scottish soldiers.

Henry's relationship with the Vatican continued to thrive. In 1521 Henry wrote a paper entitled 'In Defence of the Seven Sacraments' (*Assertio Septem Sacramentorum*), which delighted the pope so much that he bestowed the title 'Defender of the Faith' (*Fidei Defensor*) on the English monarch and his heirs. Ironically, a large part of the work concerned the sacramental nature of marriage and the supremacy of the pope. By 1530, when Henry was trying

Henry's encampment during the Battle of the Spurs, to the east of Thérouranne, was bristling with the latest defensive artillery. Chronicles of the time list 'falcons, serpentines, cast hagbushes, tryde harowes and spine trestles'. These are types of early cannon and firing pieces. Henry himself was fairly comfortable in a wooden cabin, complete with chimney, surrounded by picturesque blue, yellow and white tents decorated with the king's beasts: the lion, dragon, greyhound, antelope and dun cow. The beasts are mythical creatures representing the genealogy of kings and queens.

to find a way to be rid of his wife, Catherine, the pope revoked the honour and excommunicated the king. They were friends no longer. Ten years later the English parliament reinstated the title, which has been given to English and British kings and queens since.

WHO WAS THE BLOODIER?

It is said that the reign of Henry's daughter, Mary, the fiercely Roman Catholic daughter of his first Queen Catherine, was the bloodiest of all. But figures show that although Mary was zealous in imposing the Catholic faith, fewer than 400 executions can be laid at her door during her five-year reign. Her father's reign saw tens of thousands of men and women put to death. The English chronicler, Raphael Holinshed, who died in 1580, put the figure at 72,000 during the king's thirty-eight-year reign. Even allowing for exaggeration, it seems that Henry VIII was the most murderous of all the Tudors.

Many of these executions happened after the 1536 uprisings – the so-called 'Pilgrimage of Grace'. The prelude to this northern rebellion happened in Lincolnshire on

Hollar's engraving of a portrait of 'Bloody' Mary I.
(With kind permission of the Thomas Fisher Rare Book
Library, University of Toronto)

the evening of 1 October 1936. Evensong was over in
the parish church of Louth, whose magnificent spire had
been completed just twenty years earlier. Government
commissions, ordered by Thomas Cromwell, Henry's chief
minister, were happening in the county as a justification for
dissolving monasteries and priories, collecting subsidies and
revenues, and assessing the credentials of the local clergy.
Rumour spread. Jewels and plate were to be seized from the
wealthy parish churches, it was said. Taxes were to be levied
on cattle and on christenings, marriages and burials, while
people wanting to eat white bread or capon or goose would
have to pay a levy to the king, whispered the rumour machine.
Even worse, they said, every man would have to account for

The two men who did more than anyone to help Henry achieve his aims of power, glory and a succession of marriages found that the friendship of kings is not all it is cracked up to be. Cardinal Thomas Wolsey and his protégé Thomas Cromwell each rose to favour and high office through sheer hard work, inspired thinking and giving the king the results he wanted. But both fell out of favour, Cromwell losing his life to the executioner's axe and Wolsey dying on his way to face the wrath of the king.

Hollar's engraving of a portrait of Thomas Cromwell. (With kind permission of the Thomas Fisher Rare Book Library, University of Toronto)

all his property and income. Things reached boiling point at Louth that evening, where the people refused to accept the establishment of the Church of England. The great silver cross was taken from the altar, the church was safely locked and the keys handed to shoemaker Nicholas Melton. He became known as 'Captain Cobbler', one of the leaders of the rebellion, together with the local priest. The protest, involving as many as 40,000 people, including a sprinkling of local gentry, spread to Caistor, Market Rasen, Horncastle and other towns, culminating in a march to Lincoln Cathedral. It fizzled out when threatened by forces led by the Duke of Suffolk. Captain Cobbler, the priest and other ringleaders were hanged.

At about the same time the Pilgrimage of Grace, led by London barrister Robert Aske at the head of 9,000 'pilgrims', convened in York. Aske arranged for the monks and nuns, expelled from their monasteries and priories, to return and he organised the resumption of Catholic observances. The royal leaders, the Duke of Norfolk and Earl of Shrewsbury, found themselves facing almost 40,000 people when they met to negotiate. Following the king's instructions, these negotiators promised a general pardon and a reprieve for the monks and nuns until the next parliament. But when yet another uprising welled in Cumberland and Westmorland, led by Sir Francis Bigod, things turned really nasty. The leaders of all the rebellions were captured, convicted of treason and executed.

❧ PROTESTANT ZEAL ❧

Edward VI, Henry's long-awaited son by Jane Seymour, was just 9 years old when his father died in 1547. The intelligent and well-educated boy-king's tutors were radical Protestants, who wished to press for a complete reform of the Church. Henry, while making a complete break from the papacy and establishing Royal Supremacy, had tried to tread a middle

Hollar's engraving of a portrait of Jane Seymour. (With kind permission of the Thomas Fisher Rare Book Library, University of Toronto)

way, preserving the ancient ceremonies of the religion. But as Edward grew into his reign, he and his councillors began to use the Supremacy to impose advanced Protestantism on the country. Crucifixes, stained-glass windows and images were smashed and torn down. Paintings were whitewashed (incidentally preserving many of them), traditional religious processions banned, books and papers dealing with the 'old' religion were burnt, while the royal coat of arms replaced holy crosses on church walls. Candles, holy water, relics and rosaries were forbidden. The Mass was to be said in English, as laid down in the new (1549) Book of Common Prayer, written by England's first Protestant Archbishop of Canterbury, Thomas Cranmer.

A whole way of life was swept away. Guilds and chantries, schools and hospitals linked to the old religion were closed and many ordinary people felt exposed to the threat of hellfire. So the people rebelled. Uprisings in Devon, Cornwall and Norfolk were ruthlessly suppressed with some hangings and executions.

But Edward's most vehement critic was his own half-sister Mary, daughter of the cast-aside Catherine, and as steeped in Roman Catholicism as was her mother. How was he to deal with her open celebration of the old religion which she would no doubt impose once she became queen? Edward had to face that question much sooner than he would have liked. By the time he was 15 years old, it became clear that he was dying of tuberculosis and he was determined to prevent Mary from inheriting the Crown. So he drew up a 'device' – a document excluding his sisters, Mary and Elizabeth, from the succession on the grounds that they were both bastards. He then appointed his Protestant cousin, Lady Jane Grey, to be his successor.

🌸 BACK TO THE OLD RELIGION 🌸

Mary, the first English queen to rule in her own right, vowed to return the country to Catholicism. She became engaged to Philip of Spain, an advocate for the papacy and the Catholic religion. But the idea of a Spanish king was anathema to many. A Kent landowner, Thomas Wyatt, was one of the leaders of a rebellion in 1554 against the union and, for a while, Mary's throne seemed to be in trouble. But Mary, every inch as determined as her father, made a tremendous speech to win over her people and crushed the revolt. The ringleaders were executed and, just in case there was more trouble, she managed to implicate her half-sister Elizabeth in the rebellion, sending her to the Tower.

She and Philip were married in Winchester Cathedral, where Mary harked back to earlier days, promising to be 'bonny and buxom in bed and at board'. Now she knew that she must produce an heir in order to establish a settled Roman Catholic dynasty. In 1555, the year that the 37-year-old queen proclaimed her pregnancy, the real persecution of the Protestants began, with the terrible burning alive of men and women at the stake, including Archbishop Thomas Cranmer and Bishops Hugh Latimer and Nicholas Ridley. Mary lost credibility when it became clear that her pregnancy was a phantom and when a bill, designed to confiscate the considerable property of Protestant exiles, failed to get

Poor Lady Jane Grey did not ask for the Crown – and lost her life because of it. Edward's so-called 'device' went against his father's will and the Act of Succession. Besides which, Mary was having none of it. When Edward died on 6 July 1553 she lost no time in proclaiming herself rightful Queen of England and prepared for an armed assault on London. Those supporting Lady Jane caved in and Mary saw the throne as her own – given by a Catholic God. Jane, just 16, was eventually executed in February 1554.

Jane Grey's signature may famously be seen on the room in which she was held at the Tower. (THP)

into the statute books. Her husband disappeared across the Channel. Three years later she became dangerously ill, although she maintained to the last that she was expecting a child – again. She died, childless, at the age of 42 on 16 November 1558, leaving the throne, as her father had specified in his will, to her half-sister Elizabeth.

❀ A MODERATE SETTLEMENT ❀

For years Elizabeth, a Protestant, had been the focus of Mary's suspicion and, at times, anger. She knew that if there had been any evidence against her during the 1554 rebellion, when she was incarcerated in the Tower, Mary would certainly have ordered her execution on charges of treason. Now she had to establish a moderate Church of England and, as her father before her, tried to tread a middle way through the minefield of religion. She allied with the Protestants and, by a narrow margin, achieved her religious settlement and the acceptance of Royal Supremacy. She had to give way by allowing the introduction of Cranmer's second (1552) Book of Common Prayer.

Throughout her reign Elizabeth was pressed to marry to ensure a settled succession. The thought of no named monarch and the civil war that would surely follow was parliament's worst nightmare. If she would not marry she must name an heir – the most obvious being her cousin Mary Queen of Scots, granddaughter of her aunt Margaret, her father's sister. But Elizabeth knew that the naming of an heir would be courting disaster as that person would become the focus of any plots against her and a constant danger to her own life and the throne of England. Her advisors and parliament asked her specifically to exclude the Catholic Mary Queen of Scots from the succession. The memories of Bloody Mary's attempts to enforce Catholicism on the people were still too fresh.

She sharply reminded parliament of the time that her life as 'second person' (i.e. heir to the throne) had been in

AN ORDRE

for Mattyns daylye through the yere.

The preest beyng in the queer shall begynne wyth a loude voyce the Lordes prayer, called the *Pater noster.*

OURE father whiche arte in heauē, hallowed be thiname. Thy kyngdome come. Thy wyll be done in earth as it is in heauen. Geue vs thys day oure daily bread. And forgeue vs oure trespasses, as we forgeue theim that trespasse agaynst vs. And leade vs not into temptacion. But delyuer vs from euell. Amen.

PVBLIKE BAPTISME

When there are childrē to be Baptised vpon the Sonday, or holy daye, the parentes shall geue knowledge ouer nyght or in the mornyng, afore the beginning of Mattyns to the curate. And then the Godfathers, Godmothers, and people, with the children, muste be ready at the churche doore, either immediatly afore the last Canticle at Mattens, or els immediatly afore the last Canticle at Euensong, as the Curate by his discrecion shal appoynte. And then standing there, the preeste shall aske whether the chyldren bee Baptysed or no. If they aunswere. No. Then shall the preeste saye thus.

DEare beloued, forasmuche as al men be conceyued and borne in sinne, and that no man borne in synne, can enter into the kingdom of God (except he be regenerate, and borne a newe of water, and the holy gost (I beseche you to cal

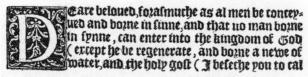

Specimens of the first Book of Common Prayer. (THP)

constant danger. She gave a hard stare around the room and narrowed her eyes, saying that she knew many of those present had been among the plotters and that only

Mary Queen of Scots was forced to flee that country after a scandal in 1568. She sought protection from Elizabeth, who had been trying to avoid any decision regarding her wayward cousin. For twenty years Mary was imprisoned in England, being moved from castle to castle and becoming implicated in a series of Catholic plots against Elizabeth. Still the queen refused to punish her further. But in 1570 the pope excommunicated Elizabeth, in effect granting permission for her Catholic subjects to assassinate her. Eventually in 1586, Mary went too far in becoming involved in an assassination plot. She was tried and condemned. Even then Elizabeth dithered over her execution. But her closest advisor, Sir William Cecil, took matters into his own hands, seeing that Mary lost her head in the great hall at Fotheringay Castle.

Mary Queen of Scots in captivity. (THP)

Pitched battle against the Spanish Armada. (THP)

her honour prevented her from listing names; she then told the lords that many of the bishops among them had preached that she was a bastard. Parliament went very quiet as their queen reminded them that was treason.

Elizabeth's last and greatest enemy was her former brother-in-law, Philip II of Spain, who sent the Spanish Armada to restore the Catholic faith and power to England and to end years of English aid to the Netherlands, who were waging their own war against Spain. The fire ships of the English navy, with a lot of help from the weather, broke up the 'invincible' Armada and Elizabeth's magnificent speech at Tilbury, when she waved a sword and wore a military breastplate, has echoed down the ages:

> I know I have the body of a weak and feeble woman, but I have the heart and stomach of a King, and of a King of England too; and think foul scorn that Parma or Spain or any Prince of Europe should dare invade the border of my realm.

5

FEAST AND FAMINE

t is early in Elizabeth's reign, say 1560. The new queen is giving a feast at her court. It might be at the splendid Whitehall Palace in the centre of London, where the buildings, with their elaborately decorated gold and white rooms, spread over 23 acres, or it may be at Greenwich Palace, where she and her father, King Henry VIII, were both born.

Elizabeth's path to the throne had been an uncertain one and she has now secured her position and her court with a deliberate policy of lavish display of wealth and ostentation: music, elaborate costume, decorated barges, fireworks and, to the horror of a foreign visitor, dancing until after midnight. And there was the food, as magnificently prepared, displayed and decorated as everything else in sight.

As Elizabeth and her principal guests make their way towards the beautifully decorated dining chamber, the musicians signal their arrival with a loud but harmonious welcome on trumpets, shawms and sackbuts. The table glitters with silverware and Venetian glass, the latter a comparatively new introduction, which only the very rich are able to buy. Each diner has a silver plate, a napkin, a knife and spoon, and a glass. A small 'manchet' loaf of the

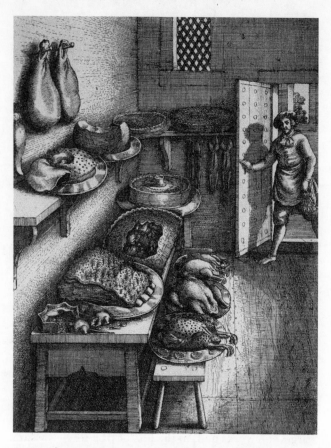

A Tudor kitchen. (With kind permission of the Thomas Fisher Rare Book Library, University of Toronto)

finest white bread is placed by the glass. There will be salt in ornate silver or gold vessels, probably fashioned in the shape of sailing ships, and boxes containing pepper, which is still a costly spice.

There is an elaborate centrepiece on the table – maybe a scene representing a smooth green lawn with trees and flowers, supporting a silver 'fortress' in which gilded birds are caged. The towers of the fortress might bear the arms of the queen.

As the queen and her guests seat themselves, a stream of servants process around the table bearing great silver platters with an astounding array – sometimes dozens – of dishes.

🌸 A DISH OF LAMPREYS? 🌸

The first part of such a dinner is the feast, with its bewildering choice, starting with, say, an offering of leg of venison in beef broth, fallow deer pasties, minced salt salmon with a sauce of mustard, sugar and vinegar, loin of veal in orange sauce, mutton pies, young goose in sorrel sauce, a pottage of sand eels and lampreys, plaice with vinegar and salt, roast lamb, swan in *sauce chaudron* (a spiced giblet gravy) or roast pig. The food is elaborately embellished with peacock feathers, colourful fruits, and gold and crimson cloth. The table might be decorated with some of the exotic fruits and vegetables from the so-called New World (the Americas), discovered in the past few decades by explorers such as Christopher Columbus and Amerigo Vespucci. Sophisticated guests might recognise pineapples and tomatoes, although they would not necessarily have tasted these exotic imports which are certainly colourful and novel enough to serve as decoration.

The musicians pick up their viols, playing soothing music of a softer tone as the guests, using their knives, select tasty morsels from the serving dishes that appear one after the other at their elbows. 'Saucers' – dishes in which the sauces are placed on the table – are set within reach and the serious business of eating starts. Well-mannered guests cut small pieces of meat away from any bones and gristle, dipping the morsels in the appropriate sauce before nibbling at them and moving on to the next dish. Anything unwanted is thrown into the 'voiders' – dishes provided for bones and sinew, peel and pips or food that does not please.

Guests at a royal feast would, presumably, have impeccable manners. Knives would be provided at such a grand occasion but they would bring their own, suitably sheathed, to a more mundane dinner. Forks would not have been provided and were rarely used, so all Tudors would automatically wash their hands before eating, in a ewer provided. Because food was picked up and eaten by hand, often from a common dish, they would refrain from poking their fingers in their ears or noses or even rubbing their hands on their hair. Men were taught not to scratch any part of themselves while at table. You did not blow your nose or wipe sweat from your face with your napkin and you certainly didn't put food back on the serving platter after chewing the meat from the bones. It was also considered extremely bad mannered to 'release wind'.

❀ CUSTARD TARTS AND FINE WINES ❀

There is a pause between courses before it all starts over again, with another procession of seemingly endless dishes carried to the table. The second course might offer peacock in wine and salt, pigeons, flounders in pike sauce, pheasant cooked in salt water with sliced onions, a dish of larks, sturgeon, crayfish or shrimps in a vinegar sauce, rabbits in a mustard and sugar sauce or a young heron in a mustard and vinegar sauce. Baked fruits will almost certainly be on the menu at this stage of the feast. There will probably be a custard tart, too, and an elaborate jelly, not wobbling in a bowl, but a brightly coloured decoration, shaped to resemble flowers, fruit, a crown or animals.

The queen will offer fine wines to her guests and she will serve it in glass – and not simple English glass, green-tinged because of the use of fern leaves in its making. Her glass, in 1560, was likely to be the Venetian glass mentioned earlier, imported from the glass blowers of Murano. The import of these fine glasses was banned after 1575 because her majesty granted a twenty-one-year monopoly in glass making to Giacomo Verzelini, whose London workshops, at the Hall of the Crutched Friars in Aldgate, produced exquisite drinking vessels, delicately engraved with hunting scenes and mythical beasts.

Wine has to be imported, being no longer made in England; therefore, by the time import duties and transport costs are paid, it is expensive. Elizabeth might serve a claret from Gascony and a white wine from France or a sweeter 'Rhenish' or Rhineland wine. Sack, popular throughout the Tudor era, is a dry, deep golden wine from Spain, often drunk with the addition of sugar, while hippocras is a sweetened wine, spiced with ginger and cinnamon, and popular with the English. Her guests might also enjoy sweet muscatel and malmsey wines, the former from France and the latter from Crete.

🌸 AND NOW FOR THE BANQUET 🌸

After another decent interval comes the 'banquet', the pudding course to end all pudding courses. The musicians strike up a more lively tune as guests rise from the table for the theatre of spun sugar confections, glistening in the light of tapers and candles, great dishes of preserved and candied fruit, sugared almonds and 'march pane' (marzipan) creations in startling colours and of all shapes. Elizabeth loved sweet, sugary food (it is said her once-fine teeth became black in middle age because of the amount of sugar she consumed) and guests gasped at one of her banquets when they were confronted with an entire zoo of spun sugar animals from camels to lions and snakes, frogs to dolphins, not to mention attendant mermaids and unicorns.

In 1508, just before the death of Henry Tudor, Wynkyn de Worde, printer and publisher, complied *The Boke of Keruying* (*The Book of Carving*), which helps us to understand the complicated rituals and etiquette of Tudor feasts in great houses and palaces. The book explains in great detail how to set out a feast, and the skills that should be learned by the servers and carvers who waited on the tables. It also acted as a handbook for the well-born pages who served the most important guests. The instructions include:

> Place the salt on the right side of your Lord's seat, and the trenchers [square wooden plates, with a depression in the middle and often a tiny hollow at the side for holding salt] to the left of the salt. Then take the knives and arrange the loaves of bread side by side, with the spoons and napkins neatly folded by the bread. Cover your bread and trenchers, spoons and knives, and set a salt cellar with two trencher loaves [flat bread that could function as a plate] at each end of the table …

The marzipan sweetmeats, moulded to represent animals, birds, flowers or trees, are coloured with saffron and egg yolk, spinach or even the copper mineral azurite to give a rich blue. Gold leaf is used, too. Music is played as the guests are free to move around while they nibble and pick at the sugary delicacies on offer.

✹ COMMON FARE ✹

Bread was eaten with every meal, but again the quality varied enormously depending on whether you were rich and could afford to eat 'manchet' (a small round white loaf made with the top-grade flour) or 'cheat bread' (a lower quality white loaf). There was also an unrefined brown loaf which had none of the bran removed and was eaten with butter. The very poor made do with bread made from maslin (a mixture of wheat and rye) or rye and barley. In times when the harvest failed, bread was baked from anything to hand – from acorns to peas and beans with oats thrown in. It was not just a case of making do; in Tudor times the poor died in their hundreds during a series of bad harvests, the worst being during the famine of 1594–97 when men walked miles from their homes looking for food and work, only to find on their return that their entire family had perished from starvation.

A soup, or 'pottage', boiled in a cauldron over the fire, was the daily fare of the labouring classes when times were not so hard. There might be a little meat – some chicken from the henhouse or bacon, maybe – boiled up with cabbage, onion, peas and beans from the garden and given some extra flavour with garlic and some more substance with a few oats thrown in. Thyme and parsley were commonly grown and used regularly for extra flavour. In winter the newfangled carrots and well-established parsnips and turnips were staple pottage ingredients. Fruit such as apples and pears, blackberries and cherries were gathered and kept as long as possible.

All classes avoided water unless they knew it was from a pure source. Beer or ale was the drink of choice, even at breakfast, when weak ale, known as small-beer, was sometimes spiced with mace or nutmeg. The wealthy sometimes drank wine at breakfast as well. Mead, which is honey fermented with water, and its herby counterpart, metheglin, was sometimes taken, while country people would opt for the much cheaper apple wine, which was a form of cider or perry. Although the yeomen and upper classes ate lashings of cream and butter, they would not touch milk. That was a staple drink for the poor.

◉ MIDDLE-CLASS RECIPES ◉

The middle classes, from wealthy merchants to yeomen farmers, ate scaled-down versions of the diets enjoyed by the very rich. Their dinners and suppers were served with a lot less fuss and ostentation. They would provide the range of meats expected if entertaining, offering their guests pigeon, heron, rabbit, hare, chicken, quail, woodcock and lark. Venison only appeared on the table if a rich friend, who was allowed to hunt deer, had sent some as a gift. When the household was dining alone, they might have started dinner with a soup and some salt beef and then maybe roast meat served with bread, some fruit and the ever-popular custard tart.

The dinner or supper was generally prepared by the woman of the house with the help of a female servant, while the householder himself carved and served the food for the family, who ate their meals in the hall or dining chamber.

In the last half of the sixteenth century, as literacy increased, 'receipt' books began to find their way into middle-class kitchens. *A Propre new Boke of Cokery* (anon.), *The Good Huswifes Handmaid for Cookerie in her Kitchen*, *The Good Huswifes Jewell* (both by Thomas Dawson) and *Mrs Sarah Longe her Receipt Booke* were all popular among those who could read. John Partridge, who published his *Treasurie of Commodious Conceites and Hidden Secrets* in 1573, found he had to run to eight editions before publishing an enlarged version in 1600. His recipe for a chicken pie sounds tantalising. He advised that the chickens should be trussed and their feet removed, before they are laid into a 'coffin' (a raw pastry case). A handful of gooseberries and a 'quantity' of butter should be added for each chicken before throwing in a 'good quantity' of sugar and cinnamon, with sufficient salt. The pie should then bake for an hour and a half. When it is done 'take the yolk of an egg and half a goblet of verjuice [crab-apple juice] with sufficient sugar sodden together, and serve it ...'

At the beginning of the Tudor era, the rich ate few green vegetables (which went under the general name of 'herbs') and fruits. Many thought them injurious to health and fit only for the poor, although the wealthy would countenance onions, garlic and leeks. But as explorers came back from the Americas and travellers returned from Italy, France and Spain with reports of the food they had eaten, the richer Tudors considered 'sallats', made with any combination of coleworts (kale), lettuce, garlic, chervil, rampion, onions, sage, fennel, leeks, borage, mint, rosemary, cucumber, parsley and watercress to be quite acceptable. They dressed their salads, as we do today, with a mixture of olive oil, vinegar, sugar and salt. Cauliflowers, pumpkins, carrots, parsnips and cabbages were all grown and imported by the end of Elizabeth's reign. Turnips, it seems, have always been with us. Tomatoes were viewed with suspicion, grown for their red beauty and decorative value and then given to the pigs to eat.

❁ FAST DAYS AND FISH ❁

A lot of meat was eaten in Tudor England – but only on certain days. Throughout the reigns of Henry VII and his son, Henry VIII, the old medieval practice of avoiding meat on Wednesdays, Fridays and Saturdays, and throughout Advent and Lent, lapsed. But in 1549 the Protestant son of Henry VIII, young Edward VI, set down in law that Fridays and Saturdays should see no meat eaten. His sister Elizabeth went further; in 1561 she ruled that Wednesday should be a meatless day too. Her reason was more practical as she was trying to support the fishing industry. However, there were ways

Fishing, from a collection printed by Wynkyn de Worde. (THP)

round these new secular laws. If you had the money you could buy a licence that allowed you to eat as much meat as you liked on any day of the week. Lords and ladies had to pay £1 6s 8d, knights and their wives 13s 4d and everyone else 6s 8d. But, although there were heavy fines and, in theory, imprisonment for those flouting the law, by 1593 the fines were lowered and many people dropped their fasting habits.

Herrings – smoked (kippers) and pickled – and dried or salted cod were available all year round. They were caught off Iceland and preserved, so could be carried for miles to sell and were very popular, as were oysters, which were comparatively cheap and eaten in pies or as they are today. Eels were cheap, too, and made into pies with wardens (pears) or apples, pepper, cinnamon, cloves, mace and sugar. A quarter of a pound of butter was added to the mix and the cook could, if preferred, thicken the whole with an egg yolk and verjuice.

Those who lived by the sea could rely on plentiful supplies of gurnard, turbot and mullet, while others enjoyed pike, roach and tench from rivers or lakes.

Butter was used lavishly in cooking and at the table, while cheese, generally eaten only by the poor at the beginning of the sixteenth century, had become accepted as a tasty addition to dinners and suppers by the end of the century.

A WOMAN'S WORK ...

Many yeomen and middle-class households were largely self-sufficient in providing food and clothing for the family and servants. And this is where the wife of the householder would be firmly in charge.

Delights for Ladies, a book written by Sir Hugh Platt, was published in 1609, six years after the death of Queen Elizabeth. But the role of the 'huswife' had not changed in that short time and the book gives some idea of the enormous tasks facing women running Tudor households and of the produce, food and materials they were expected to provide for their families. This book was republished in 1948 with an introduction by Kathleen Rosemary Fussel, who points out that these women, keeping account of everything spent and everything produced, achieved a list of daily activities that were 'legion'. The women baked the household bread and brewed the beer, they churned the cream to make butter and ground meal for the table. They not only bred and cared for the animals – cows and sheep – that they would eventually eat, but were also responsible for the slaughtering and the butchering. They looked after the henhouse and collected the eggs. They carried out or oversaw the spinning of their wool and flax to make fabrics. There was needlework (fine and coarse) embroidery, cooking, curing, preserving and distilling, all to be supervised by the lady of the house. They organised the vegetable garden and made herbal

A 'huswife' might decide to cook a dinner of salmon and 'taffaty tarts' on a non-meat day. She would first wash her salmon in a little vinegar and water, letting it 'lie a while' before putting it into a 'great Pipkin with a cover' (an earthenware cooking pot with a handle and three small feet). She would add six spoonsful of water, four of vinegar and white wine, a 'good deal' of salt, a handful of sweet herbs, some white sorrel, cloves, a little stick of cinnamon and some mace. 'Set it [the Pipkin] in a Kettle of seething [boiling or simmering] water, and there let it stew three hours.' She is advised that 'Carps, Eeles, Trouts' may also be cooked thus.

Her 'taffaty tarts' would be made with a butter and cold water 'Past' (pastry), which she must 'Rowle very thin, also then lay them [apple slices] in layes, and between every lay of Apples strew some Sugar, and some Lemon Pill, cut very small, if you please put some Fennell-seed to them; then put them into a stoak hot Oven ...' After an hour or more, she would remove the tarts to cover them with a mixture of rosewater and butter, and sprinkle with sugar before warming them through in the oven prior to serving.

remedies and medicines. These women, who ruled the domestic business of the household, were never anything but busy, preserving, conserving, candying, making syrup, jellies, beatifying washes, mouthwashes, pomatum (fruit) essences, vinegar and pickles.

⬢ TIME TO EAT ⬢

As today, there were no set meal times in Tudor England, but, as a general rule, breakfast would be taken early – between six and seven o'clock – while dinner, as the main meal of the day, was served at eleven in the morning in rural areas and country towns. More sophisticated Londoners ate their dinner at midday, followed by a six o'clock supper, rather than the five o'clock meal taken by their country cousins.

Breakfast became a regular meal in Tudor times. Historians say that people in medieval England rarely ate

The Manner of sitting at Dinner of Ferdinand Prince of Spanie, on the day of his Invethiture.

Holy Roman Emperor Ferdinand II (1578–1637) feasting at his investiture in the Order of the Garter. (With kind permission of the Thomas Fisher Rare Book Library, University of Toronto)

an early morning meal but certainly, by the beginning of the sixteenth century, bread and butter (sometimes with the addition of sage leaves to sharpen the intellect), some weak beer and perhaps some fruit would be eaten by country people. Servants, too, ate bread and butter for breakfast, but their loaves would not often be the fine white 'manchets' of the better-off, but the grey-looking 'cheat' bread. The gentry might eat a pancake stuffed with currants and sprinkled with sugar, or some salt fish or pickled herring to go with their mugs of ale or wine. The very poor would break their fast with some rye and barley bread enlivened by an onion or a piece of cheese.

❀ PREPARING FOR WINTER ❀

Food was seasonal and depended heavily on the harvest. What was not used must be preserved for winter – and there were some shockingly cold winters in what some historians and climatologists have called the 'Little Ice Age', when the Thames regularly froze over.

If you were a farmer or landowner with herds and flocks of animals, you could slaughter them for meat at any time, but, if your animals were few and too expensive to feed during the winter, the cows, sheep and pigs would be butchered and their meat preserved by dry-salting – burying in granular salt – or cured in brine. Salt was expensive so the former method was used only for the best meat. Sometimes a sea salt from Brittany was used but this was often contaminated with sand, seaweed and grit, turning it into a suspicious greyish-green colour. It was so coarse that decay had already set in by the time the salt penetrated the inner part of the meat. The most common method of preservation was to cure joints and sides of meat in a strong saltwater solution. Meat that was known to be tough and stringy was not preserved as it wasn't 'worth its salt'.

The vast quantities of food served at Tudor feasts might seem wasteful but in fact every scrap of it was used. When the platters came back into the kitchens, the staff had first choice of what was left. The rest was often divided between the almshouses and the hospital (buildings for the homeless and very sick), and those begging at the gate. Anything remaining would be fed to the pigs.

Fish, on the other hand, was well worth the trouble. Herring was plentiful and cheap and, although oily, as long as it was salted or cured as soon as it was caught, it would last a good while. Cod, too, discovered by English sailors in the North Sea, were huge fish and salted and dried in quantity. When there was a requirement to fast (that is, to eat no meat) during Advent and Lent, herring and cod, preserved in this way, helped make meals seem less tedious.

Simply soaking the salty meat or fish did not disguise the taste, so Tudor cooks devised dishes that needed plenty of salt themselves and that would be cooked with the salted beef or cod to absorb the excess brine. Most commonly that would be done by preparing dried beans or peas or whole grains, or even breadcrumbs, pureeing them or leaving them whole. Sometimes baked fruits and spices or even a good jugful of cream would be added to disguise the salty flavour.

The preserved meat and fish might be served with frumenty, a pudding-like side dish made with cracked whole wheat, boiled with milk and eggs or broth and sometimes flavoured with almonds, sugar, saffron and currants. It was commonly served with venison as well.

Alternatively, it might be turned into 'mortrews' (mortar-paste) of fish or white meat boiled and pounded to a paste before being combined with breadcrumbs, stock or almond milk and eggs, and cooked again until stiff enough to slice, and served with the addition of a little pepper and ginger.

Cooks, who had not the ingredients or the time to make their own sauces for rendering salted foods palatable, could buy these delicacies from professional sauce makers, who would offer a yellow sauce made with ginger and saffron, a green sauce that was also flavoured with ginger but with the addition of green herbs, cardamom and cloves or a more exotic cameline sauce. This was made by pounding together 'raisins of Corinth' with nuts, breadcrumbs, powdered ginger, cloves and powdered cinnamon before binding it with a little vinegar and salt.

Fruit was carefully stored, too. Only the flawless apples and pears were kept. Still carrying a length of stalk, they were laid carefully, none touching the other, in the 'hoard house' or 'apple house' on mats of clean straw. They were turned, equally carefully, each month, to ensure that there was no damaging moisture underneath. Householders were urged to lock the doors of the hoard house 'lest children make havoc there'.

Soft fruits were preserved in jams and marmalades but, again, this was something only the wealthy could afford to do, as the necessary sugar was expensive and a lot was needed to ensure that the jams and jellies, made with gooseberries, quinces, cherries, plums and damsons, did not go mouldy over the winter.

6

PEOPLE AND PLACES

ngland's landscape changed gradually over the Tudor period as taxes, laws and new building materials altered the way people lived.

Henry VII did not like other people's castles. They seemed too much to be the enclaves of warlords with private armies – which he also disliked intensely. Almost as soon as he became king in 1485, he saw to it, through legislation and fierce fiscal measures, that the great titled landowners, who had the potential to cause trouble if they wanted to question his claim to the throne, were subdued. Since the arrival of the Normans in 1066, castles with their distinctive battlements had been built as symbols of power and authority. The licence to 'crenellate' – to add battlements through which arrows or other weapons could be discharged – was allowed only by royal authority, but Henry was having none of that so very few licences, even to repair existing crenellations, were allowed.

Therefore no new castles were built over the Tudor reign and even the Royal Family abandoned their existing castles in favour of much more comfortable palaces and great manor houses. The Tower of London, which was essentially a castle, was no longer a real royal residence and Windsor became a castle in name only, as home comforts were installed and defence systems made redundant.

Windsor Castle. (With kind permission of the Thomas Fisher Rare Book Library, University of Toronto)

Greenwich Palace, sometimes called the Palace of Placentia or Pleasaunce, where both Henry VIII and his daughter Elizabeth were born, was a royal favourite, while nearby Eltham Palace was another. Henry VII rebuilt the fire-ravaged Sheen Palace in 1501, changing its name to Richmond and transforming it into a house of great luxury and magnificent show.

🌸 BUILDING BRICKS OF THE FUTURE 🌸

Two new materials, gradually introduced over the sixteenth century, also played a huge part in changing the shape of English architecture.

Brick was the first. The medieval hall houses, with their timber frames and one, or possibly two, large rooms open to the rafters had their hearth in the middle of the room. If you had bricks, you could build a chimney, allowing a fire on the ground floor to discharge its heat while being able to build first and even second floors with many rooms. So houses in towns became taller, grander and warmer.

The second material, available by the end of the century to the reasonably well-off, was glass. By the beginning of Elizabeth's reign, some rooms in many houses were glazed, letting in light while fending off cold draughts. The supreme example was the glorious renaissance-style Hardwick Hall in Derbyshire, built by Robert Smythson, stonemason and architect for the redoubtable Bess of Hardwick in the late 1590s. Bemused visitors exclaimed at the extraordinary expanse of glittering glass, a powerful indication of Bess' wealth, leading to the tag, 'Hardwick Hall, more glass than wall!'

Throughout the fifteenth century and at the beginning of Henry VII's reign, most large establishments had followed the same pattern. Castles, manor houses or palaces had a great hall, longer than it was wide and featuring, across the width

Bess of Hardwick (Elizabeth Shrewsbury) was the richest woman in Britain after Queen Elizabeth. Each of her four marriages had brought her enormous wealth which she displayed conspicuously in her many mansions. Another of her great houses was Chatsworth in Derbyshire, the principal seat of the Dukes of Devonshire, Bess' descendants. Born in 1527, Bess, the daughter of a Derbyshire yeoman family, married first at 14, was widowed within the year and then married the rich Sir William Cavendish with whom she had eight children. When Sir William died she remarried and was widowed again before marrying the wealthiest man in the country, the 6th Earl of Shrewsbury, with whom she fought bitterly until their separation in 1584 and his death in 1590. She died enormously wealthy and in possession of many houses.

at one end, a fixed or movable screen. The screen passage behind led to the service areas – kitchens, buttery (larder) and the pantry. Sometimes a gallery which overlooked the hall was built above the screen. At the upper end of the hall, facing the screen, was the high table, usually standing on a stage or raised platform, where the owners and their guests sat to dine and to conduct business. At right angles to this table were others, running the length of the hall.

A private living room, known as the 'solar', opened off the hall by way of a door behind the high table. Beyond this often richly furnished and decorated room were the family's bedrooms and accommodation for their guests. Another wing housed the many servants necessary to keep even a modest establishment running smoothly. There would also be cellars and other storerooms, stables, granaries and barns.

The advent of brick and glass was of no benefit at all to the working classes, whose cottages, wherever they were in the country, did not change much throughout the whole Tudor period. Small, draughty and dark two-room, single-storey cottages were the norm in rural areas, although the material with which they were built varied according to the geology of the region; you would find cob (a mixture of clay, sand, straw, earth and water) in Devon and Cornwall, limestone and sandstone elsewhere and many timber-framed buildings in the Midlands and Cheshire because of the lack of suitable stone.

By the middle of the Tudor period (from about 1520–60) the larger houses were losing all resemblance to castles, but they kept something of the old courtyard pattern, albeit on three sides only.

❀ The Rise of the Prodigy House ❀

Comfort and luxury – and more than a touch of ostentation – became apparent as great palaces or 'prodigy houses' appeared, built at first by the Royal Family and then by

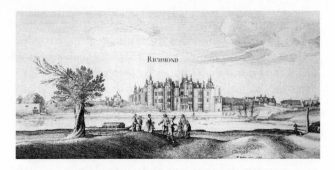

*Richmond Palace. (With kind permission of the Thomas
Fisher Rare Book Library, University of Toronto)*

Some of the early examples of the change in
direction of English architecture can be attributed
to John Morton, a lawyer and clergyman who went
on to become Bishop of Ely and, later, Archbishop
of Canterbury, and also trusted chancellor to
Henry VII, devising punitive systems of taxation to
raise revenue for the king.

In the two last decades of the fifteenth century
he built a great palace at Hatfield in Hertfordshire.
The Royal Palace of Hatfield, seized by Henry VIII
at the time of the Dissolution, was the childhood
home of both Queen Elizabeth I and her young
brother, Edward, who later reigned for six years as
Edward VI. It was here that Elizabeth was living
when she was told that her half-sister Mary had
died and that now she was queen. Not much of
the palace remains today. When the 'new' Hatfield
House was built nearby by the 1st Earl of Salisbury
in the first decade of the seventeenth century,
he kept the magnificent hall to use as his stable,
demolishing the rest of the palace. That hall has
now been restored to some of its former glory.

other wealthy families, who expected at some point to entertain the royal household. This great undertaking was viewed by the prospective hosts with equal feelings of dread and pride. Pride that they had been chosen as worthy hosts for the greatest in the land and dread at the cost and considerable disruption that entertaining royalty always caused. So these rich courtiers, determined to do things properly, began to build great mansions opulent enough to entertain the king or queen in style and large enough to accommodate the huge retinue required by the royals as they made their progress round the kingdom.

Richmond Palace, built by Henry VII, his son Henry's Nonsuch Palace in Surrey and Hampton Court, built in the first instance for the eventually disgraced Cardinal Wolsey and later appropriated and enlarged considerably by Henry VIII in 1529, were all in the 'prodigy' league – all designed by an architect (often the ubiquitous Robert Smythson) to be original and individual. So too was Hardwick Hall in Derbyshire and the beautiful Longleat House in Wiltshire, still inhabited by the Thynne family who commissioned it in 1567.

ROYAL SHOW HOUSES

The Tudors, the new dynasty, led the way in building great show houses. Today all that remains of Henry VII's magnificent Richmond Palace, on the south bank of the River Thames 9 miles upstream from Westminster, is the gatehouse and a couple of streets bearing the names 'Old Palace Lane' and 'Old Palace Yard'. But people marvelled as Henry, once the Earl of Richmond, changed the name of the old Sheen manor house to reflect his title, and he tore it down to build his new luxury home at the beginning of the sixteenth century. The town of Sheen took the much classier name of Richmond too. The new palace was built to encompass the latest in

European architecture and design. The great glass bay windows set into redbrick walls, glittered, reflecting the river light, while fourteen onion-shaped, lead-covered domes shouted majesty and wealth. Acres of pleasure gardens, filled with topiaried trees, orchards, bowling alleys, tennis courts and archery butts, were there for entertainment while, inside, long covered galleries invited talkers and strollers to take exercise when the weather was inclement. Rich furnishings, tapestries and statues filled the halls while everywhere was carved the Tudor 'brand' – the red and white rose, the red dragon and the portcullis, the indelible stamp of Henry's authority. Richmond was the beautiful setting for the final celebrations following the wedding of Henry's son, Arthur, the Prince of Wales, to the *infanta* Catherine of Aragon in November 1501. The palace was enjoyed by Henry's heirs. His granddaughter, Queen Elizabeth, who had spent many exciting days stag hunting in the park there, was taken to Richmond Palace – which she called her 'warm box' – in January 1603. She died there two months later, in the early hours of 24 March.

Tudor palace Hampton Court (seen here around 1797).
(Courtesy of the Library of Congress, LC-USZ62-107796)

Henry Tudor's son and successor loved the luxury of building great showy palaces too. When Henry VIII went to stay in the magnificent state apartments at the enormous newly built home of his Lord Chancellor, Cardinal Thomas Wolsey, in 1525, he was not best pleased. There was nothing at all wrong with the wonderful palace at Hampton Court, which could house a retinue of 500, had cost the unimaginable sum of 200,000 gold crowns to build and was clearly the most glorious palace in the whole of the country. Wolsey, flamboyant and with an irrepressible and theatrical sense of display, kept a court here at least as fine as any presided over by the king. Henry, who owned sixty or so great houses, had nothing as magnificent as this and he was, frankly, jealous. Three years later Hampton Court with its great inner courts (Clock Court, Fish Court, Lord Chamberlain's Court, Master Carpenter's Court and Round Kitchen Court) was his. Wolsey, failing to secure Henry's divorce from Catherine of Aragon, was out of favour, and so, willingly or not, he handed his wonderful home to his master as a gift.

The famous and rare Hampton Court astronomical clock built into the tower overlooking Clock Court, which housed the state apartments in Tudor times, was carefully constructed by clockmaker Nicholas Oursian in 1540–41. A Bavarian astronomer, Nicolas Cratzer, is said to have designed it. It tells the hour, month, day of the month, the position of the sun, the signs of the zodiac and the phases of the moon, including the hour in which it passes the meridian. In so doing, it also tells the time of high tide at London Bridge – very useful for the Royal Family who often travelled between royal palaces by barge. The clock was restored to full working order in the early twenty-first century.

Henry, conscious that his new palace could become large enough to house his entire court of more than 1,000 people, ordered that the kitchens should be made four times larger. Then he built the enormous medieval-style great hall with its hammer-beam roof and elaborate stonework, which took a team of masons working round the clock, sometimes by candlelight, five years to complete. Henry also built his tennis court here.

St James's Palace, another grand home built by Henry VIII in the 1530s, is, confusingly, still the official residence of the British sovereign, although no monarch has lived there for almost 200 years. It is, however, the official London residence of several senior members of the present Royal Family. It is also home to the Court of St James, where every ambassador and high commissioner arriving in the country is received and accredited. The palace, in Pall Mall, was named for St James the Less, to whom a leper hospital once on this site, disbanded in 1532, was dedicated.

All accounts emphasise that the favourite royal residence of all the Tudors was that great house built at Greenwich. This glorious palace, whose beautiful grounds swept down to the bank of the Thames, was the best-loved royal home for more than 200 years. It pre-dated the Tudors, being seized in 1447 by Margaret of Anjou, wife of King Henry VI, from its owner the disgraced Duke of Gloucester who had called it Bella Court. Margaret quickly renamed the imposing residence the Palace of Placentia. At the beginning of the sixteenth century, Henry Tudor revamped the palace, developing the new rooms around three great courtyards and laying out glorious gardens and a large hunting park. Like his other palace at Richmond, it was easily reached from London by royal barge.

❀ THE PALACE OF PLACENTIA ❀

Henry VIII was born at Greenwich Palace, or Placentia, and spent much of his childhood there with his mother,

Elizabeth of York, who loved the place. Later, when he became king, he spent vast amounts of money on making further improvements and building armouries, stables and a new banqueting hall. He also commissioned a huge new tiltyard, or jousting ground, which was situated below two high, brick octagonal towers so that spectators could watch the games taking place below. Henry, in his youth an accomplished horseman and a star at the joust, suffered a serious accident at Greenwich during a tournament in 1536. His horse fell and rolled on to him as he lay injured on the ground. He was unconscious for some time and never jousted again.

Much that was significant in the lives of the Tudor Royal Family happened at Greenwich. Henry married two of his wives – Catherine of Aragon and Anne of Cleves – at the palace, while both Mary, his daughter by Catherine, and Elizabeth, Henry's daughter by Anne Boleyn, his second wife, were born at the palace. Unhappily for Anne Boleyn, it was here that she was arrested, accused of adultery, incest and treason, and here that Henry signed her death warrant before she was beheaded outside the Tower of London on 19 May 1536. Henry's son, who reigned as Edward VI, died at Greenwich in 1553.

Queen Elizabeth had happier memories of Greenwich, keeping a regular court here, although she made Whitehall Palace in the heart of London her main residence. Here her bedroom, overlooking the Thames, was sumptuously decorated with a gold ceiling and a bed expertly made with different woods and covered with quilts of velvet and silk, embroidered with gold and silver.

Greenwich Palace eventually became a naval hospital before being converted to house the Royal Naval College. The site of the old palace is now part of the University of Greenwich but virtually nothing of Tudor times remains.

Henry VIII had happy times, too, at nearby Eltham Palace, where he and his sisters lived when not at Greenwich during early childhood. Unlike his brother, Arthur, who was groomed for monarchy for most of his short life, Henry was allowed more freedom and fun during his boyhood and Eltham, with its substantial parks and gardens, provided the setting for the royal children's games.

Now the great Tudor hall, complete with hammer-beam roof, has been restored but today's visitors go to see the lavish 1930 Art Deco home of Stephen and Virginia Courtauld, built in the bailey of the medieval palace.

Hollar's engraving of a portrait of Anne of Cleves, who married Henry at Greenwich. (With kind permission of the Thomas Fisher Rare Book Library, University of Toronto)

Greenwich was the palace of choice for Anne Boleyn to have her baby in 1533. But she had to follow the strict rules laid down for royal mothers-to-be, where the confinement was literally that. She was sent into seclusion in a suite of rooms which included a great chamber, a birthing chamber and an oratory with a font, in case the newborn ailed, needing immediate baptism. All males, even the king, were excluded. Her women took on traditional male duties such as those of pantry men and butlers. Escorted by high-born ladies, Anne was taken to her oppressively dark and stuffy bedchamber. Tapestries covered walls, the ceiling and even the windows. A thick carpet was laid and keyholes and any aperture that let in the tiniest glow of light were covered. The great bed, with a wool-stuffed mattress, fine linen sheets and large feather pillows, was ready for her. Alongside were two cradles: one the formal state cradle, upholstered in red and gold and with a crimson and ermine counterpane to match that on the queen's bed, and another 'cradle of tree' made of carved wood, painted gold. With braziers burning and open bottles of scent perfuming the air, the room was stuffy and claustrophobic. The rules dictated that confinement should begin four to six weeks before the expected date of delivery. Anne, probably pregnant before her wedding on 25 January 1533, went into labour on 7 September, giving birth to Elizabeth, a healthy baby girl.

Hollar's engraving of a portrait of Anne Boleyn. (With kind permission of the Thomas Fisher Rare Book Library, University of Toronto)

'THE FIRST WELL-BUILT HOUSE IN ENGLAND'

Many of the great prodigy houses, built by courtiers and gentry to show off the wealth and position of the owner and also to accommodate a royal visit, stand today. Many of them were made possible by the fallout from Henry VIII's dissolution of monasteries and priories where land and the redundant monastic buildings were given to favoured courtiers who rebuilt or refurbished the medieval dwellings.

Longleat, in Wiltshire, is one of the finest and most complete of the great Elizabethan houses. The original building, formerly an Augustinian priory, was bought by Sir John Thynne for the sum of £53 in 1541. But it was destroyed by fire twenty-five years later and Thynne, established by this time in the court of Queen Elizabeth, decided to rebuild in the new English Renaissance style epitomised in the design of London's Somerset House. What developed, with help from stonemason and architect Robert Smythson and carefully steered by Sir John himself, was one of the finest examples of the new Elizabethan building. Longleat, when finished in 1580, just before John Thynne's death, was acclaimed 'the first well-built house in England'. Thynne did welcome Queen Elizabeth to his home, although the visit was made in 1574, several years before it was finally completed.

Robert Smythson, whose input on the exterior design was considerable, is referred to today as an 'architect', although the profession had not been clearly defined in Elizabethan times. Smythson, born in 1535 during the reign of Henry VIII, was a first-rate stonemason. By the time Elizabeth was on the throne, he was travelling around England with his own team of masons, working on the great mansions that were becoming fashionable. During the 1560s he moved to Wiltshire where, for almost the next two decades, he worked on Longleat for the Thynne family. He is known to have carried out much of the exterior stone carving and to have had considerable input into the overall design of the house. At least three of the other great Elizabethan houses, Hardwick Hall in Derbyshire, Wollaton Hall, prominent on high ground in Nottingham, and the beautiful brick-built Burton Agnes near Driffield, East Yorkshire, are all built to his design. He died at Wollaton (now a museum) in 1614 and was buried in the church there. His memorial refers to him as an 'Architecter'.

❀ LOST MONASTERIES ❀

One of the most important events in Tudor history was the Dissolution of the Monasteries, ordered by Henry VIII to quell any chance of these great establishments harbouring those, disgruntled at the new powers he had assumed, who might rise up against him. He also realised that some of the enormous wealth accruing to the monasteries and their vast estates might do very nicely in his treasury. Between 1536 and 1540, more than 850 monasteries and priories were suppressed, some giving in gracefully and others struggling to survive. Those monasteries not razed to the ground have survived as ruins, such as the Benedictine monasteries

Two of the best preserved of the suppressed monasteries are great Yorkshire establishments. At remote Fountains Abbey, near Ripon, can be seen the ghostly outlines of the 300ft-long dormitory with its storeroom underneath. Rievaulx, built on the tree-lined banks of the River Rye near Helmsley, was founded, like Fountains, in the 1130s by the Cistercians, inspired by the teachings of St Bernard of Clairvaux. Constructed in early Gothic style with pointed arches, Rievaulx has the remains of an almost complete refectory and parts of the dormitory.

at Lindisfarne and Glastonbury or the Augustinian ruins at Colchester in Essex or Kirkham in Yorkshire. Others, such as the early thirteenth-century Augustinian priory at Mottisfont in Hampshire, were converted to secular use, while some retained their churches which were put to use by the local town or parish.

❀ ROYAL MEMORIALS ❀

However, as the Royal Family takes away, so it also gives. Churches, chapels and educational establishments were founded throughout the reign, mostly as memorials. In 1503, the year that his wife, Elizabeth, died in childbirth, Henry Tudor made a down payment of £30,000 for the building of an exquisite Lady Chapel in Westminster Abbey. The chapel, said to be the last great masterpiece of English medieval architecture, was probably designed by master masons William Vertue and Robert Janyns. It is approached by a flight of stairs and guarded by finely made bronze gates, embellished with Tudor emblems. Above is a wonderful stone fan-vaulted roof, resplendent with carved pendants. Dozens of saints, carved in stone, line the walls to guard the magnificent tomb of Henry and his queen, Elizabeth of York, which lies behind the altar. Henry's mother, Margaret Beaufort, outlived her son by a few weeks and, as in life she was never far from the seat of power, so in death there is a monument to her in the south aisle of the chapel.

Margaret was responsible for the foundation of two Cambridge colleges, Christ's and St John's, and so her grandson Henry VIII took over payment for the completion of the glorious King's College Chapel at Cambridge. Work on the chapel had been carried out in fits and starts under Henry VI in the 1440s, about sixty years earlier. Henry VII gave funds for work to resume in 1506, but it was under the reign (and purse) of his son that the chapel, which has the largest area of fan-vaulted ceiling in the world, was

> Visitors to Trinity College, Cambridge, with its fabulous Great Court and Wren Library, are often surprised to see that the statue of its founder, King Henry VIII, standing in splendour over the entrance gate appears to be brandishing a chair leg instead of a sword. This is the result of a student prank many years ago.

completed, although the great windows were not finished for another fifteen years.

Henry also re-founded Christ Church in Oxford, the college intended by Cardinal Wolsey to be his grand memorial (using funds from dissolved monasteries to pay for it). But when the disgraced Wolsey fell out of favour, the king seized his properties, including Wolsey's Cardinal College, renaming it in the process. At the same time, he ordered that the partly demolished priory church here should be rebuilt as the cathedral of the city of Oxford. Not liking to do things by halves, he also merged two existing Cambridge colleges, Michaelhouse and King's Hall, into the splendid Trinity College.

At both universities Henry established Regius professorships in civil law, Greek, Hebrew, theology and medicine, and he endowed eleven cathedral grammar schools with some of the proceeds of the Dissolution.

7

Movers and Shakers

evolutionary changes in political thinking, science, religious practice, literature and the arts in general happened not only in England in the sixteenth century, but also across Europe. This was the time when the West emerged from the medieval age to begin an exploration of the earth and its place in the universe. It was an era when science made real advances in medicine, engineering, navigation and astronomy. In 1543 the Polish mathematician and astronomer Nicolaus Copernicus published his revolutionary and, to some, blasphemous, theory that the earth was not the centre of the universe, but just another planet orbiting the sun. That heralded the beginning of modern science.

In England, the political landscape shifted with the advent of the Tudors. Henry VII, who had bided his time to grab his kingdom, now bound it to him and his heirs with iron ties. His new laws forbidding private armies and reinforcement of castles ensured that it would be hard for any aspiring warlord to topple the new dynasty; he reinforced those laws with punitive taxation. His son, seeking to establish the succession with a male heir, founded the Church of England and his granddaughter, Elizabeth, presided over the so-called 'golden age', when thinkers, writers, explorers and scientists flourished. Thanks to the introduction of printing to England by William Caxton less than ten years before Henry Tudor became king, the means to disseminate the new ideas was well established.

But kings and queens do not make laws or rule without help. Each of the Tudors relied on councillors and advisors – the political movers and shakers of the age.

❀ CHURCH AND STATE ❀

The Lancastrian Henry Tudor would probably not have aspired to the throne at all had it not been for the machinations of two ambitious women, his mother, Margaret Beaufort, and his future mother-in-law, Elizabeth Woodville, widow of the Yorkist Edward IV. Elizabeth's two sons, Edward and Richard, would have succeeded but for the fact that they were probably murdered by their uncle Richard, who went on to seize the throne. Margaret, who had waited fifteen years for the chance for Henry to take the kingdom, plotted with the understandably vengeful Elizabeth Woodville to marry Henry to Elizabeth's daughter, so that the warring houses of York and Lancaster would be united, as Henry made his bid to fight for England by defeating the usurping Richard III in battle at Bosworth Field. Once Henry was crowned, his mother did the dirty on her former friend. Margaret, never far from the seat of power, saw to it that Elizabeth Woodville's lands and properties were confiscated and the former queen was sent to live in a nunnery, even though she was the new king's mother-in-law.

Henry's chancellor, John Morton, had served as Master of the Rolls and Bishop of Ely under Edward IV but had opposed Edward's successor, Richard III, who had had him flung into captivity in Brecknock Castle for his disloyalty. His fortunes were restored by Henry Tudor, who made him Archbishop of Canterbury and Lord Chancellor –

John Morton died in 1500 and was succeeded as Henry's chief advisor by Bishop Richard Fox, who not only successfully negotiated the marriage of Prince Arthur, Henry's son, to Catherine of Aragon, but was just as wily as John Morton in devising methods of collecting revenue. Thomas More, later Sir Thomas, scholar, lawyer, statesman, author of *Utopia*, and upholder of the Catholic faith, served as a page boy in the great house of Archbishop Morton. He later became convinced that Fox was the evil genius behind the tax collection system known as 'Morton's Fork'. Fox's power did not wane during the early years of Henry VIII's reign: the Venetian ambassador called him '*alter rex*' (the other king), although Henry let slip to Carroz, the Spanish ambassador, that his advisor was aptly named 'a Fox indeed'.

with the brief to build up the country's exchequer. Morton was more than equal to the task and devised tax systems that left the treasury bulging, but also left a nasty taste in the mouth (and a big hole in the purses) of his people.

❖ LOSING THEIR HEADS ❖

Sir Thomas More rose to power during the reign of Henry VIII and opinions divide on whether More's persecution of Protestants when he was Henry's chancellor was justified, but all historians agree that he was a scholar and learned man of letters without rival. He teetered between the law and a religious calling but opted for the former. He remained a devoted and aesthetic Roman Catholic, wearing a hair shirt and practising flagellation. His insistence that his intelligent daughters be educated to the same standard as his sons amazed many, but inspired

Thomas More and his daughter in the Tower. (THP)

others to do the same. His publication *Utopia*, sometimes described as the first science-fiction novel, describes and compares the imaginary island state of 'Utopia' with early sixteenth-century Europe – to the detriment of the latter. It paved the way for many other fictional descriptions of ideal states. More, unable to accept Henry's supremacy over that of the pope as head of the Church, resigned the chancellorship in 1532. He was executed for treason in 1534 for refusing to swear his allegiance to the parliamentary Act of Succession.

Henry VIII's two other closest advisors, More's predecessor as chancellor, Thomas Wolsey, and Wolsey's own protégée, Thomas Cromwell, both died in disgrace. Each had used his considerable political, legal and financial acumen to give the king exactly what he wanted and, in turn, had received enormous reward – while they realised his demands. But Henry was a hard taskmaster and one failure was enough. In Cardinal Wolsey's case it was the failure to engineer a divorce between Henry

Cardinal Wolsey arriving at Leicester Abbey, where he perished shortly afterwards. (THP)

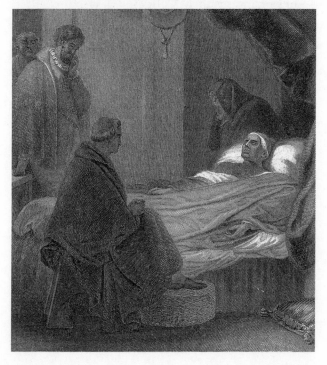

and Catherine of Aragon, so that the king could marry
Anne Boleyn. Wolsey, who was also Archbishop of York,
was stripped of his government offices and property in
1529. He travelled to York – the first time he had ever
visited 'his' cathedral city – but was recalled to London

At the height of his powers, in 1515, Wolsey,
a brilliant showman, was the supreme fixer in
matters of both State and Church. He provided
the magnificent and flamboyant outward display
that Henry loved, while dealing with all the boring
business of running the country that the young
monarch abhorred. The grandiose peace conference
between England and France, the Field of the Cloth
of Gold, was entirely Wolsey's idea. It showed off
Henry, who fancied himself as holding the balance
of power in Europe between France and Spain, as a
statesman of substance. The whole event, in a vast
open area of north-east France on 6 June 1520,
was a grand and lavish spectacle with wrestling
and jousting competitions, fairy-tale pavilions,
spectacular feasting and tents made of cloth of gold,
dotted everywhere across the immense plain.

Field of the Cloth of Gold. (THP)

to answer charges of treason. He died on the road back to the city, in great distress, at Leicester in 1530. 'If I had served my God as diligently as I did my king, he would not have given me over in my grey hairs,' the 60-year-old cardinal is said to have uttered on his deathbed. Cromwell stepped into Wolsey's shoes as chief minister and, with the help of others, especially Archbishop Thomas Cranmer, eventually achieved the king's divorce. He went on to organise a system whereby the considerable cash from the Dissolution of the Monasteries poured into the king's coffers. When the new marriage broke down, Cromwell was the fixer who managed to sever Henry's relationship with Anne – and her head too – when the king demanded it. But his failure to provide Henry with an attractive new wife (Anne of Cleves, the Flanders mare, was not what Henry wanted at all) cost Thomas Cromwell his own head, in 1540, for arranging the botched liaison.

❁ A PROTESTANT ARCHBISHOP ❁

Another fixer, Archbishop Thomas Cranmer, was also to lose his life in service of his sovereign, although that was to happen later, under Bloody Mary, Henry's daughter. A Cambridge theology don, Cranmer left the city in the summer of 1529 to avoid the plague, joining university men Edward Fox and Stephen Gardiner who had been working with Wolsey to try to achieve the annulment of Henry's marriage to Catherine. Cranmer turned the argument on its head. This was a moral issue, he said, not a legal one. Henry was enthusiastic. 'That man [Cranmer] hath the sow by the right ear!' he declared. And so it was put to experts at the English universities (that is, Cambridge and Oxford) to debate the matter and come up with a moral verdict. Cambridge decided for the king and, later, so did Oxford. Theologians across Europe debated the issue and (not without bribery and coercion)

Henry's case was defended. So the idea that the king, not the pope, should rule the Church in his own realm was born. Henry gradually forced the matter through Convocation (the governing body of the English Church), although there was much opposition. In January 1533, in secret, Henry and Anne were married. Henry, still legally married to Catherine, was now a bigamist. Anne was pregnant and the divorce must happen soon so that the child would be legitimate. Cranmer, now Archbishop of Canterbury, quickly ruled that Henry's marriage to Catherine was void. He also upheld the validity of the king's marriage to Anne Boleyn.

Cranmer, on his diplomatic travels abroad, explored his growing interest in the Protestant Reformation movement and in Lutheranism. He married, for the second time (his first wife having died in childbirth), Margaret Osiander, the niece of a Lutheran reformer. He became the architect of what is now known as the English Reformation, creating the basic structure and tenets of the Church of England. He supported the translation of the Bible into English. This was the so-called 'Great Bible', translated by Myles Coverdale, who incorporated much of the Tyndale Bible into this new version. In 1545 Cranmer composed the English litany that is still used today and, during the reign of Henry's son Edward VI, he introduced both the first and second Books of Common Prayer, largely written by himself.

Cranmer's star was still in the ascendant during the reign of Edward, the son of Henry and his third wife, Jane Seymour. By now firmly Protestant, Cranmer made it clear during Edward's coronation in Westminster Abbey, on 20 February 1547, that the young king had been chosen by God and was answerable only to the deity, thus enforcing Henry's Royal Supremacy. Edward was just 9 when he succeeded and a council of regents, led by his uncle, Edward Seymour, Duke of Somerset, who became self-appointed Lord Protector, governed in his name.

Thomas Cranmer's 1540 Bible, showing Henry VIII as the supreme head of the Church. (THP)

Under Seymour and the man who succeeded him, John Dudley, Earl of Warwick, later Duke of Northumberland, England followed an increasingly Protestant direction. Cranmer and the young king directed the stripping of church decorations and banning of ritual, processions and the saying of Mass in Latin.

Edward was almost 12 when his uncle Seymour, the Duke of Somerset, faced rebellion in October 1549 from those unhappy at his mismanagement of the country in the name of the king. Seymour, taking Edward with him, fled to Windsor Castle, where Edward noted in his chronicle: 'Me thinks I am in prison.' Seymour was soon arrested and Edward was taken to Richmond, where he wrote down the nature of the charges against his uncle: 'Ambition, vainglory, entering into rash wars in mine youth, negligent looking on Newhaven, enriching himself of my treasure, following his own opinion, and doing all by his own authority, etc.' Seymour got away with his life that time but, just over two years later, in January 1552, the teenage king's chronicle entry reads: 'The Duke of Somerset had his head cut off upon Tower Hill between eight and nine o'clock in the morning.'

Cranmer, England's first Protestant Archbishop of Canterbury, did not survive the reign of the fiercely Roman Catholic Mary Tudor. Edward, who died of tuberculosis in 1553, at the age of 15, had done everything he could to prevent Mary succeeding him but their father's will named her in the succession. The Archbishop of Canterbury was asked to recant his Protestant faith. And he did. But Mary wasn't going to let him off that easily. He was to be burnt at the stake in Oxford after making another, public, rebuttal of his views. A platform was built in the university church of St Mary's on 21 March 1556 so that everyone could see him confess. But Cranmer, ashamed of his previous weakness, magnificently repudiated his recantation and denounced the pope as the Antichrist. He was rushed to the stake and, as the flames roared up, he thrust the

Thomas Cranmer at the Tower – on 8 March 1554 he was sent to the Bocardo Prison in Oxford, where he was later executed. (THP)

'sinning' right hand that had signed the recantation deep into the flames before he was consumed by fire.

❀ A STEADY HAND ❀

The last great advisor of the Tudor era was the sober and steady William Cecil, Lord Burghley, whose political life and that of Elizabeth I were entwined. She would ask for his advice before all others and she relied on him completely. Elizabeth and Cecil trusted and liked each other long before she became queen. Cecil, like Elizabeth, trod a fine line during the reign of Mary Tudor, careful to keep his Protestant views under wraps. But, when Mary died and Elizabeth was proclaimed queen, he knew that never again should England be torn apart by Catholic rule and it was he who steered Elizabeth through a moderate religious settlement. Cecil was not a political innovator or an original thinker, but he was wise and able to guide with a safe pair of hands when England and the new and often impetuous young queen needed his wisdom. He was not completely averse to

Lord Burghley and his signature. (THP)

taking risks, though. When Elizabeth dithered over the go-ahead for the execution of the Catholic Mary Queen of Scots, refusing to allow the signed death warrant to be expedited without her further command, he took action, disobeying Elizabeth and ensuring the warrant reached Mary at Fotheringay Castle, where she was imprisoned. He would not countenance another Catholic threat to the country.

❁ MEN OF SCIENCE ❁

Life became a whole lot more complicated for everyone in the sixteenth century. Suddenly, as the English Reformation gathered pace to match that of northern Europe's Lutheran movement, the pope was seen as fallible and the structure of religious and political life changed forever. If that were not disturbing enough for the great majority, scientists and philosophers were questioning the fixed view of the earth as the centre of the universe, orbited by an obedient moon and sun, home to every living creature.

In 1543, a book by Polish astronomer Nicolaus Copernicus was published, arguing that the fixed point was the sun, while the earth, just like the other planets, merely followed an orbit around it. He was not the first; Greek and Islamic scholars had posited this theory much earlier but their ideas had been rejected or not even noticed. But another great innovation – the ability to publish ideas widely, with the invention of the printing press by Johannes Gutenberg in 1450 – had made possible the dissemination of information. And with the publication of his book *de revolutionibus orbium coelestium* (*On the Revolutions of the Celestial Spheres*) days before his death in May 1543, Copernicus' theory of a heliocentric universe was discussed across Europe and in England, although it met with strong resistance for many decades to come. One believer was English astronomer Thomas Digges, whose own observations, when he discovered a new star in 1572, agreed with the Copernican theory of the position of heavenly bodies. Digges, a distinguished astronomer, was a pupil of one of the greatest Tudor 'natural philosophers', Dr John Dee.

'Scientist' was a word not yet coined, but the sixteenth century was the time of 'natural philosophers' whose observations and discoveries led to changes in medicine, knowledge of the natural world and discovery of new lands with their different peoples, vegetables, minerals, fruit and animals.

A Welshman, John Dee, born in 1527, was a polymath – astronomer, astrologer, mathematician, navigator and alchemist. He studied science and magic with equal openmindedness. He was a consultant to Queen Elizabeth on astrological and scientific matters and an advocate

John Dee saw no conflict between his interest in mysticism and magic and his extraordinary skill as a mathematician. He spent as much time exploring his belief that humans had the capacity for divine power as he did on his calculations. In fact, he believed that this divine power could be triggered through mathematics. He was a devout Christian and spent considerable time trying to communicate with angels in a bid to improve the lot of humans on earth and to bring about a unified world religion. Although posterity viewed him with suspicion as a charlatan because of his reputation as a magician, twentieth-century research has come to the conclusion that he was a fine scholar and one of the most learned men of the late sixteenth century. It is thought by some historians that Shakespeare's Prospero, the imposing sorcerer of *The Tempest*, was based on John Dee.

of English exploration overseas in order to discover new lands and build an empire. He promoted the sciences of navigation and map making, while his mathematical and navigational skills were called on when those about to set forth on voyages of discovery needed guidance and training.

❀ THE FATHER OF ❀ EXPERIMENTAL SCIENCE

Two other Elizabethans whose reputations as natural philosophers went before them are William Gilbert (1544–1603) and Francis Bacon (1561–1626). Gilbert, a physician and physicist and one-time president of the Royal College of Physicians and personal doctor

Sir Francis Bacon. (With kind permission of the Thomas Fisher Rare Book Library, University of Toronto)

to Elizabeth I, studied magnetism and was the first to recognise that the earth was itself magnetic, with a core of iron, which was the reason that all compasses pointed north. He carried out many experiments on a model of the earth (which he called the *terella*), the results of which he published in his book, *On the Magnet and the Magnetic Bodies, and on the Great Magnet, the Earth.* He is credited as one of the originators of the word 'electricity', which he coined when he used amber in his experiments with static electricity; amber is *elektron* in Greek. He called the result of his experiments the 'electric force'.

Sir Francis Bacon, with his ever-enquiring mind, his experimental nature and his thirst for inventions to better the lot of mankind, has been called the 'father of experimental science'.

He served his country as Attorney General and Lord Chancellor and was a philosopher, scientist, author, orator and statesman. It is said he died of pneumonia while testing the preservative effect of ice on meat, but he suffered ill health throughout his life so this is probably not wholly true. He carried out many experiments himself and called for scientists not only to think about practical inventions but also to work towards making machines that would ease the daily burden of mankind.

❀ EXPLORATION ❀

This was the time of extraordinary discovery on earth as well as in the heavens. The push across the oceans to seek new lands was initiated by the Spanish and the Portuguese, with Columbus setting forth across the Atlantic in the late fifteenth and early sixteen centuries to reach the Americas. Columbus, although Italian by birth, led his fleet in the name of Spain. The Portuguese Vasco da Gama boldly sailed around Africa to the East Indies, discovering the rich spice routes that enriched his country's economy. For centuries sailors had risked their lives on the seas, but gradually improving navigational devices aided discovery in Tudor times. The accurate calculation of longitude was still out of reach, but latitude (the distance north or south of the equator) was calculable using instruments such as compass, quadrants, astrolabes and an hourglass to measure time and distance.

In 1569 the Flemish geographer and cartographer Gerardus Mercator introduced navigational charts which greatly aided the brave English seamen who were already exploring the seas with enthusiasm. Both Sir John Hawkins (whose father, one of Henry VIII's sea captains, had made a voyage to the Americas in 1527) and Sir Francis Drake were making their fortunes by shipping slaves across the seas and engaging in acts of piracy against the Spanish. Hawkins went on to become the chief architect of Elizabeth's navy, improving the design of the ships (and the pay of the mariners). Meanwhile, between 1577 and 1580, his cousin Drake achieved the first circumnavigation of the globe by an Englishman, in the *Golden Hind*, capturing and looting Spanish treasure ships along the way. On his return to Plymouth on 26 September 1580, he was able to hand over gold, jewels and spices to Queen Elizabeth, who had cannily taken a major share in the expedition, the value of which was more than the Crown's income for an entire year. Both Drake and Hawkins played major roles in the defeat of the vengeful Spanish Armada in 1588.

Queen Elizabeth knighting Sir Francis Drake. (THP)

Inventions that did indeed improve the lot of mankind, just as Francis Bacon hoped, came thick and fast through the sixteenth century. They included the first flush lavatories, graphite pencils, the pocket watch, bottled beer, navigational charts, the 'stocking frame' (a type of knitting machine), a horizontal waterwheel, the compound (or multiple lens) microscope and the water thermometer.

Sir Walter Raleigh, for a while Queen Elizabeth's favourite, was a true polymath. A flattering and witty courtier, writer, lawyer, poet, soldier, explorer, shipbuilder and historian, he left behind a slim volume of poetry, the founding of American colonies, the popularisation of tobacco (although he was not the first or only explorer to bring tobacco leaves to England) and the *Ark Royal* – a ship he had built for himself, calling it *Ark Raleigh*, but renamed when he sold it to the queen to pay off his debts. Raleigh, tall, dark and very handsome and with a fetching Devon accent, was in and out of trouble most of his life. He was given gifts of land, property and money by the queen, but fell firmly out of favour when she discovered that he had married and fathered a child by one of her ladies-in-waiting, the beautiful Bess Throckmorton. He and Bess were both flung into the Tower but were forgiven and survived to enjoy a happy marriage at their home in Sherborne – for a while. Raleigh lost his head to James I's executioner some years after Elizabeth's death.

🌼 LITERARY GREATS 🌼

At the beginning of the sixteenth century only 10 per cent of men and 1 per cent of women in England could read. By 1600, a quarter of all men and one in ten women were literate; by the time Queen Elizabeth died in 1603 more than 400,000 people could read.

Printing in English for the masses happened when William Caxton set up his printing press in Westminster in the last quarter of the fifteenth century. He died in 1492, having printed more than 100 books, including Chaucer's *Canterbury Tales* and *Le Morte d'Arthur* by Malory. More printing presses sprung up and books, from household manuals to medical, horticultural and veterinary self-help guides were available. The availability of this useful material encouraged people, men and women, to teach themselves to read, helped also by the availability of the Tyndale Bible, now printed in English rather than Latin. And those who could write did so.

Bookshops opened, despite censorship introduced by Henry VIII in 1530. Throughout the Tudor reign, all books were vetted by six members of the Privy Council, while the sovereign's Master of Revels had to approve each play before its performance. The old religious mystery and miracle plays that were standard fare in Roman Catholic England were now banned but, despite Puritan opposition, a flood of new tales poured from the pens of playwrights, keen to enthral with tales of history, love, murder and betrayal. The queen was present at the Inner Temple for the opening of the first play to employ blank verse. *Gorboduc*, the story of a kingdom torn asunder by two heirs, enthralled the audience, who were well versed in those sorts of dramas.

Theatres were built and the populace was hooked. Thomas Kyd's *The Spanish Tragedy* (1587) and Christopher Marlowe's *Tamburlaine the Great* (1587/88) spoke to the masses. The passion deployed on stage with great set-piece speeches and action, replacing the old ritual, was exciting and engaging. Ben Johnson managed not only to get himself arrested for his slanderous and offensive first play *The Isle of Dogs* (co-written with Thomas Nashe), but also to have every theatre in London closed. But they soon re-opened

Shakespeare. (THP)

and Johnson's less-than-promising start was followed by a smash hit, *Every Man in his Humour*.

Johnson, Marlowe and Shakespeare are the three great names from a long and distinguished list of dramatists putting on plays during the sixteenth century. And they were prolific. Each of these three had written at least six plays before he was 29. And each had something new to say, showing the enthusiastic audience that their feelings and the conditions they endured or enjoyed were universal and true and belonged to all human beings, whatever they may have been told by Church or State.

❧ MUSICAL INTERLUDES ❧

Music flourished, too. Henry VIII employed more than fifty musicians and enjoyed his own orchestra (or consort) of harp, dulcimer, pipe, trumpet and tabor (a snare drum played with one hand). He owned many instruments and played and composed himself, while his daughter, Elizabeth, who had about thirty players in her household, was more than proficient on the virginals (a keyboard instrument). Lutes, flutes, citterns and viols were played by many, and music for dancing and songs was not only composed but printed and published.

Suddenly new musical fashions emerged, and first came the jolly madrigal, for three to six voices. Popular musicians of the day, such as Thomas Weelkes and John Wilbye, wrote

There was still a ban on the public performance of religious motets and masses, although this sacred music continued to be composed by men like Thomas Tallis, Dr John Bull and William Byrd. Tallis' famous motet, *Spem in alium*, was certainly performed, but only behind closed doors in private chapels.

many of them, while even the traditional court composers, including William Byrd, condescended to pen one or two. Then John Dowland, the brilliant exponent of the lute, and Thomas Morley started composing 'airs' – ethereal and plaintive, lilting and lovely songs for a single voice. All these composers and others worked together and singly to feed the ever-growing hunger for instrumental music of all sorts, performed at private functions, public gatherings and, quite often, during performances of dramas by the greatest of playwrights, William Shakespeare, who often felt a play wasn't quite the thing without a little song or two inside.

8

KEEPING UP
APPEARANCES

THE QUEEN IS DRESSED

 am no morning woman,' declared Elizabeth I, refusing to do business with anyone or to see any male member of her household until she was up and dressed – which could take a couple of hours. But often, before the lengthy task of getting ready to face the day, she would take an early morning walk in the gardens of whichever palace she inhabited at the time.

Always accompanied by her retinue of ladies, she still wore her nightclothes for these pre-breakfast strolls and she must have revelled in striding out in the comparative freedom of her loose gown, which would have been made of costly taffeta and velvet, or silk, elaborately decorated and lined.

Back in her rooms at Greenwich or Whitehall, her ladies would see that her bathtub was full of warm scented water, or would help her to wash with linen cloths dipped in brimming pewter bowls. Her teeth scoured with cloths, it was time to start the daily ritual of dressing, which would take at least an hour and often more to complete. Over her fine cambric linen shift would be fastened, pinned and stitched her 'bodies': the two parts of the wraparound 'bodice', laced at the back and front and stiffened with whalebone. Elizabeth had bodies of silk, satin and velvet, and at least one made of perfumed leather. Tudor women did not wear drawers. Stockings would be smoothed on to the royal legs and a petticoat might be attached to the 'bodies', or she might wear a embroidered kirtle – that is, a full length petticoat, often with sleeves, designed so that the front was seen underneath the opening of the gown. That would be slipped over her head to fit on top of the 'bodies'. She might also

A young Elizabeth I, from her portrait at Westminster. (THP)

wear a forepart or stomacher to cover her undergarments if her gown was slashed open very low at the front. The queen favoured jewel-studded white satin stomachers for maximum effect. A farthingale, the whalebone framework that gave shape to her gown, was put into position and fastened. Farthingales, using up to 50 yards of whalebone, had to be light in weight but strong enough to support petticoats and an elaborate gown.

Then came the gown itself, fastened with hooks and pins or laces or carefully stitched on to the undergarments (and equally carefully unpicked before bedtime), adorned with ruffs and lace. An inventory of Queen Elizabeth's clothes and jewels, made in 1600, shows she owned almost 350 gowns alone, in a variety of styles, from the French gowns with trains, which had to be carried by a servant, to 'round' gowns with wide hems. These latter were open at the front to show off her kirtles and stomachers. She also owned loose gowns, normally sleeveless and straight. Her flashier 'Spanish' gowns had artfully slashed sleeves to show off the colours of the garments underneath.

The inventory shows that, following the new fashion of the 1570s, the queen owned and might have worn a doublet, or its sleeveless equivalent – a jerkin. Both were garments that mimicked menswear and caused outrage among the more Puritanical male population.

Queen Elizabeth, like all other wealthy women, had to make do with fine knitted linen stockings for the first part of her reign. But a breakthrough came in 1561 when, at the New Year celebrations, her silk woman, Alice Mountague, triumphantly presented her with a pair of knitted silk stockings. They were not easy to make – it took Mrs Mountague ten years to make the first pair. In 1599 William Lee invented his knitting machine, which gave other wealthy people access to fine silk stockings.

Clothing of the period of Elizabeth I. (THP)

The 'head on a plate' fashion for wearing ruffs, popular with both sexes, developed in the middle of the century, from the custom of showing a little bit of the collar of your smock, shift or shirt over the neck of your gown or doublet. This soon developed into a linen ruff band, independent of the undergarment.

❀ BEING WELL SHOD ❀

In 1562 Queen Elizabeth granted a third Royal Charter to the Guild of Cordwainers, the shoemakers who had supplied the wealthy with their fine leather shoes and boots since before the accession of Henry Tudor in 1485. The guild, which was also granted arms by the queen in 1579, had grown from the ancient companies of leatherworkers who used the finest and softest leather, which came from Cordoba in Spain and was made from goats' skin. It was called 'cordwain'. Those craftsmen making shoes and boots retained the title 'cordwainers'. The queen would have owned supple Spanish leather shoes, but she could also have chosen from soft velvet slippers ('slippers' because they can easily be slipped on and off) or pantofles – a fancy French title for a slipper, worn by men and women alike, with a padded leather sole and a decorative finish on the leather or velvet upper.

It is interesting to note that leather or wooden shoes were never worn when playing tennis on an indoor court, lest their creaking should distract the players.

For special occasions, shoes of satin and taffeta were worn with the part of the sole that touches the foot brightly coloured with scarlet. Mules or chopins were chosen for outings; their wooden soles were a couple of inches or more high, to keep the wearer's foot from the mucky ground, although they had velvet or leather uppers. Chopin wearers often needed the support of a friendly arm to keep them from falling from their elevated platform shoes. Pumps were often worn by lackeys because these supple, thin-soled, leather slip-ons allowed the wearers to walk quietly without disturbing those they served.

Men's shoes were of uniformly sized leather, fitting snugly over the foot, often with no fastening. Sometimes a cut was made in the leather on the outer side so that it could be buttoned back down or tied with a bow or buckle.

It became the height of fashion during the last part of the sixteenth century to decorate footwear for dances, feasts or banquets with 'shoe roses'. At first ribbons were looped to mimic the Tudors' favourite flower, but refining touches saw the roses fashioned from gold and silver lace.

Working men's shoes and boots were made of leather, too, but of the cheaper, harder quality, shaped into short boots with thick soles or stouter ones reaching to mid-calf. Gamaches and buskins – long boots of the softest leather – were worn by the wealthy. At the very beginning of the Tudor era, shoes were finished with pointed toes, but by the turn of the century, they were more comfortably rounded to follow the shape of the wearer's foot.

❂ STYLES FOR MEN ❂

Throughout the Tudor era, the doublet and hose dominated male fashion, but the styles changed over the period. A doublet was a front-fastening, lined jacket, normally with sleeves, worn over a shirt of cambric or silk. Buttons or laces held it together. Hose, or 'hosen', was the general term for breeches, stockings and anything else a man might wear below the waist. In the early part of the century, breeches and stockings were made in one piece but, by the 1570s, they were fashioned as separate items, allowing for a great deal of variation from the elaborate and decorative galligaskens and round hosen made from velvets and damask, to the tighter and more revealing knee-length Venetians. The galligaskens widened out around the thighs and fastened neatly, often with a frill, just below the knee. Round or French hosen were

The overt display of masculinity evident in men's clothing of Henry VIII's reign had largely disappeared by the time his daughter, Elizabeth, came to the throne. The huge overstuffed codpieces popular at Henry's court had disappeared altogether, although some smaller examples were still to be seen, while the wide, padded doublets with heavily accentuated shoulders, denoting male strength and power, were not the type of fashion to flaunt at the court of the Virgin Queen.

The masculine costume of the time of Henry VIII. (THP)

rounded, too, but finished mid-thigh, the fabric ballooning over the point at which they were fastened. Stockings called 'netherstocks' covered the lower leg.

Working men might have worn doublets and hose of inferior materials but some simply put on a shirt covered by a cassock-like garment, the whole pulled together with a belt.

❁ EARLY FASHION ❁

Men, unlike women, did wear drawers. At the beginning of the era men would don braies or slops made of linen, resembling a closely fitting part of shorts. By the middle of the century, the better off were opting for the newly fashionable longer and looser linen undergarments, embellished with silk embroidery and hanging, from pleated gathers at the waist, down to mid-thigh. Boys and the working classes did not bother with drawers at all – they simply tucked the tails of their shirts between their legs. All shirts, again mostly made of linen, were long, falling to the thighs, with slits in the sides so those who did not want or could not afford to wear drawers could tuck them through their legs for comfort and hygiene's sake.

Fashion for high-born ladies right at the beginning of Henry VII's reign, from 1485, was simpler and more modest. The medieval cut of gowns, all in one piece, was giving way to a bodice and skirt of the same material but separated at the waist, the join covered by a belt or scarf of a contrasting colour. The bodice fitted snugly and was cut square at the neck with an embroidered and sometimes jewelled band, which would continue down the length of the dress at the front. Peeping coyly above the decoration was the frilled edge of the fine cambric or lawn undergarment or shift. The sleeves were long and tight with deep cuffs of velvet or even fur, a decoration repeated on the hem of the long skirt which trailed, train-like, at the back. On a State occasion the royal

A working man of this time wore thick cloth hosen and stout shoes, the two often united by the addition of cloth gaiters, tied under the knee and above the ankle. Over his undershirt he would wear a tunic, buttoned in the front and tied at the waist with a piece of cloth, twisted and shaped to form a useful carrying pouch. He would wear a basin-shaped hat of rough felt or even straw, sometimes over a skullcap of thinner material.

or noble lady would wear a full-length mantle, richly embroidered with her armorial bearings. Headdresses at this time were modest and nun-like rather than elaborate, and are now known as Tudor gables to reflect the way they fell around the face.

❖ PRACTICAL WOMEN ❖

Middle-class women opted for simplicity, wearing square-necked sleeveless gowns over an under-robe of contrasting colour. The under-robe was full in the sleeve, while the gown displayed a deep band of velvet, often black, which was an expensive colour to achieve, around the neck. The armholes were finished with a similar, if narrower, velvet band.

A working-class woman would still wear a one-piece gown of cheaper woollen fabric, laced at the front where the neck was cut square or scooped in a round shape. The straight sleeves hung loosely enough to be rolled back up the arm when she had to undertake household chores such as washing clothes or scrubbing vegetables. The skirt of her gown might fall almost to the ground or could have been cut short, to reveal a longer, contrasting, underskirt or petticoat. Working women, especially those who had to be outside, would not want to be constantly trampling on the hems of their gowns. Hoods of linen, twisted and tied to suit, were worn as head coverings, while everyday shoes would have been made from leather or felt.

Showing acres of cleavage, even a near-bare bosom, was perfectly acceptable behaviour for unmarried women, but any lady showing bare arms or legs would have been courting scandal.

CUTTING YOUR CLOTH

There were no artificial fabrics in Tudor times but there were mixtures of silks, linens and wools, and cloth was bought and worn according to income and status. In fact, laws were in place to prevent people from wearing materials above their station. Cloth was important in sixteenth-century England and the fabrics that people wore and the styles they chose told everything about their place in the Tudor hierarchy.

The best and most expensive fabrics were those worn by royalty and the very rich, who had their pick of velvets, satins, silks, damask, taffeta, sarcenet and grosgrain. Then came linens, the finest being lawn, cambric and holland, all pure white and used for making shirts and smocks, ruffs and aprons. Lawn, in particular, was so fine that it was used for ruffs, fine cuffs and partlets (neckerchiefs). Lockram, canvas and buckram were used by middle-class men and women for their shirts, whilst poorer men and women used a fabric called 'linsey-woolsey', a hard-wearing linen and wool mix.

Rich clothes of Edward VI. (THP)

Wool fabrics were legion – after all, a major part of the English economy was the wool trade – and cloth merchants or mercers could reel off a dozen or so types of fabric made from this most useful of materials. There was scarlet, broadcloth, scammel, frizado (a scarlet wool) and kersey at the top end, moving to the middle range of russet, frieze, kendal and cotton (a lightweight wool, nothing to do with pure cotton). Flannel, worsted, bay and serge were also types of woollen fabric.

The very rich would have relished wearing their gowns and doublets in cloths of gold and silver or even crimson cloth of gold, expensive fabrics woven with a warp of pure gold or silver and a weft of silk. The crimson version would be woven with crimson silk to give an effect of shimmering, sumptuous colour. Other expensive mixes included tinsel (silk and gold or silver thread mixed), camlet and cyprus, both silk and linen weaves. Mockado, fustian and linsey-woolsey were all cheaper wool mixes.

The Tudors inherited medieval laws, dictating who could wear what. In theory, heavy fines were imposed for those daring to wear an outfit above his or her station. Rules laid down by Henry VIII in 1533 decreed that only peers of the realm (and royalty of course) were allowed to wear cloth of gold or silver, tinsel, sable (a fur) or satin mixed with precious threads. Those wanting to wear the shining black furs of genet (a mongoose-like mammal related to cats) or lynx, woollen cloth made abroad or red or blue velvet must be lords, the sons or daughters of an earl, a Knight of

A bizarre law brought in by the Wool Cap Act of 1571 ruled that fines of 3s 4d should be paid by all those working people above the age of 7 years who did not wear a woollen cap each Sunday and holy day. The fine should have been imposed for each day the rule was ignored. But, as with the rules dictating forbidden fabrics for certain classes, the infringements were so widespread that most transgressors got away without their woollen caps.

the Garter or a marquess. Velvet gowns and coats, leopard furs and embroidered clothes of any sort were permissible only for lords and their sons, knights or anyone with an annual income of more than £200. And those unfortunate enough to have income below £100 a year could not wear clothes of satin, taffeta or damask, or outer garments made with silk, some clothes made of velvet or the fur from native wild animals. But so many people, tempted by the luxury of fine fabrics, disobeyed the rules that fines were rarely imposed.

THE KING'S CLOTHES

When Henry VIII achieved the throne in 1509, he was a young, athletic, handsome man. Contemporary descriptions of him, his clothes and considerable style show that he remained conscious of his fine figure and good looks for many years before he became obese and unhealthy. Foreign ambassadors and diplomats attached to the Tudor court made regular lengthy and detailed reports back to their own countries, which reveal much about the lifestyle of the Tudor royals. A Venetian diplomat, visiting Henry's court during the first quarter of the sixteenth century, was a man named Pasqualigo who took care during his visit to study Henry, his clothes, his apartments and his deportment. In 1515, when Henry was in his early twenties, the Venetian describes being ushered into the king's presence after a river trip on a royal barge to Richmond Palace where Henry received him and his delegation. The king was leaning against his gilt throne, where the long gold sword of state lay on its cushion of gold brocade. Overhead was a canopy of cloth of gold, made in Florence ('the most costly thing I have ever witnessed,' writes the overawed Pasqualigo). He describes his host's gorgeous apparel, noting first a cap 'of crimson velvet ... and the brim was looped up all round with lacets and gold enamelled aiglettes' (small hanging fastening tags). The king wore a doublet, described as 'in the Swiss fashion' with alternate stripes of crimson and white satin. His scarlet hose were slashed carefully from the knee upwards, the silk stockings cut and stitched carefully back above the thigh to reveal another, probably contrasting, layer underneath. To complement this colourful and fashionable outfit, Henry wore a purple velvet mantle, sumptuous with a white satin lining and the sleeves 'open with a train verily more than four Venetian yards in length'.

A young Henry VIII, in his splendid clothing. (THP)

The mantle, or thick cloak, was fastened across the breast with a thick gold cord 'from which there hung large glands, entirely of gold ...' These 'glands' were ornamental loops through which the gold fastenings would be secured.

But it was the rich variety of Henry's jewels that really excited his guest: 'Very close round his neck he had a gold collar, from which there hung a rough-cut diamond, the size of the largest walnut I ever saw, and to this was suspended a most beautiful and very large round pearl.' Pasqualigo also noted a 'very handsome gold collar' over the mantle, from which hung a 'St George entirely of diamonds'. Beneath the mantle, the king wore a dagger covered by a pouch of cloth of gold 'and his fingers were one mass of jewelled rings'.

In contrast to the fashionable outfit worn to impress foreign diplomats, Henry would dress down for a game of tennis (or 'tenes'), of which he was inordinately fond. Another Venetian, the ambassador Sebastiano Giustiniani, sent home a description of the athletic king playing his favourite game: 'he is extremely fond of tennis, at which game it is the prettiest thing in the world to see him play, his fair skin glowing through a shirt of the finest texture.'

Henry would have worn a fine cambric or lawn shirt with a finely decorated square neckband. His shapely legs (of which he was extremely proud) were bare and his 'slops', or little shorts, made of silk or velvet with 'cuttes', or small slashes, outlined with gold cord, finished with a gathering band around his upper thigh. He had two 'tenes cotes' of black and blue velvet to throw over his shoulders after a vigorous game.

❁ AND SO TO BED ❁

Nightgowns and nightshirts came into their own in Tudor England. In medieval times there were no special garments designated for sleeping in, apart from the ubiquitous nightcap. Women would keep on the chemise they had worn during the day or replace it with the clean one they would wear the next day. Men could choose to wear a shirt or nothing at all (except for the nightcap). When staying at an inn or away from home, bed sharing was not unusual so men would generally keep their 'braies' (undershorts) on, but there was no hard and fast bedtime etiquette.

By the time Henry VIII was on the throne most men wore a nightshirt, which evolved from the usual long day shirt to a special one for sleeping in. Unlike the day shirt, which had ties to attach the ruff, the sleeping shirt had a collar,

often with ties for drawing it snugly across the neck to keep
out any harmful draughts or chills. A miniature, painted
in 1534, shows a 'goodlie young lord' wearing his collared
nightshirt complete with three linen ties. The shirt, which
seems to be of white linen, has full sleeves. The young man is
Henry Fitzroy, Duke of Richmond, Henry VIII's natural son
by Elizabeth Blount. Fitzroy was the only illegitimate child
ever acknowledged by his father, who bestowed wealth and
honours upon him. Fitzroy (meaning 'son of the king'), who
was 15 when the miniature was painted, is also wearing a
'nightbonet' – a close-fitting skullcap that completely covers
his hair – made of white linen and embroidered with designs
in black silk. Sadly, Fitzroy died when he was 17.

Records, made a couple of years before this portrait was
painted, show that Henry ordered 'a nightgown' in black
satin and taffeta for 'the Lady Anne'. This was for his love
at the time, Anne Boleyn, not yet his mistress or his wife,
but soon to be both. The nightgown of Tudor times was
the equivalent of today's dressing gown, made long, loose
and open to wrap over and fasten at the front.

Henry VIII's second queen, Anne Boleyn, may
not have been popular among the people of
England – they called her 'the King's Whore' or a
'naughty paike' (prostitute) – but she did know,
to her dying day, how to dress. On 19 May 1536,
she climbed the scaffold erected outside the Tower of
London. She was turned out perfectly as she always
had been. Her gown was of grey brocade and had
very full sleeves, turned back and was covered with
grey squirrel fur, which also trimmed the front of her
skirt. The skirt was cut away to reveal an underskirt
of rose-pink satin. She wore, as usual, a French
hood. On this day the hood was of black velvet,
decorated with pearls.

Nightdresses, or 'nightrailes', did not change much through Henry's reign to that of Elizabeth, being made of materials such as fine cambric, embroidered with silk and often perfumed. By the time Queen Elizabeth was on the throne, many men owned nightgowns as well, to serve as dressing gowns to keep out the chill while waiting to get dressed or washed.

Slippers for bedroom use were not unknown, either. A household account for the Earl of Northumberland, who died in 1527, lists: 'night buskyns of rede leder and black cordwyn, furred with black lambe' (bootees of red and black leather, with cordwyn being the best quality Spanish leather) trimmed with black lamb's wool.

❀ HAIRDRESSING ❀

How your hair was cut and styled was almost as important as the way you dressed. A contemporary account of an Elizabethan barber shop complains about their:

> strange fashions and monstrous manners of cuttings, trimmings, shavings and washings, that you would wonder to see ... and therefore when you come to be trimmed, they will ask you whether you will be cut to be terrible to your enemy, or amiable to your friend, grim and stern in countenance, or pleasant and demure (for they have divers kinds of cuts for all these purposes, or else they lie).

Before the razors came out, 'rubbers', or linen cloths for the purpose of freshening up the hair with a good hard rub, were brought out and used. Then several ivory combs, each more fine-toothed than the last, were pulled through the tangled locks. Men always carried their own combs of ivory or wood with differently spaced teeth so that the hair could be tidied and any nits or other unpleasant hangers-on

Beards in the Tudor era. (THP)

got rid of. Beards and moustaches were treated likewise, although those preferring a clean-shaven look would need the attentions of a barber at least twice a week.

Before Elizabeth's reign, most women's hair was dressed simply – pulled back from the forehead but the side teased forward and rolled up slightly. But when the red-haired queen flaunted her frizzy locks everyone wanted blonde, auburn or golden hair, and they dyed their own with anything to hand, from the reasonably gentle chamomile, lemon juice and saffron to the more corrosive and harmful sulphur powder. Elizabeth piled her curly hair high on her head – probably to stop it catching in her elaborate ruff – and the fashionable of the time did the same, combing their hair back over pads to give it height. They even plucked hair to imitate her high forehead and used hot tongs to make frizzy curls.

Wigs for both sexes were widely used. Towards the end of her reign Elizabeth owned dozens of wigs which she matched with her outfits, hiding the loss of her once-fine head of hair from the public.

9

CONCLUSION

he Tudors came from almost nowhere to claim the English throne and, despite danger from all quarters, established a glorious dynasty that changed the face of monarchy.

Henry Tudor brought an end to the often troubled 330-year rule of the Plantagenets, defeating the Yorkist army of Richard III at Bosworth in 1485, killing the king to seize the crown for himself and putting a stop to the on-going Wars of the Roses.

Without a secure base or a large army, Henry relied on oppressive legislation to curb the power of the nobles and raise enormous amounts for his exchequer. Methodical and dour, he ensured that the monarch ruled absolutely.

The sovereign became a 'king emperor' and 'defender of the realm', under Henry Tudor and his flamboyant son, Henry VIII, whose quest for an heir saw him, rather than the pope, head of the English Church.

Henry VIII inherited a bulging treasury, a revitalised navy and a secure monarchy. But he wanted a male successor which meant a divorce from his Spanish wife, Catherine. Out of the ensuing conflict with the pope arose the Church of England with Henry, and future sovereigns, its supreme governor.

The long and mainly peaceful reign of his younger daughter, Elizabeth, the last Tudor sovereign, saw a

Protestant monarchy firmly established and a newly literate people absorbing the ideas brought by the writers, scientists, explorers and inventors who flourished during the late sixteenth century.

Above all, the royal supremacy established by Elizabeth's father and grandfather had been preserved. Even today our institutions, from the Church, to parliament, to universities and the Armed Forces, still offer allegiance to the sovereign.

FURTHER
READING

Borman, Tracy, *Elizabeth's Women: The Hidden
   Story of the Virgin Queen*, Jonathan Cape (2009)
   (Vintage edition, 2009)
Helm, P.J., *Exploring Tudor England*, Robert Hale (1981)
Mortimer, Ian, *The Time Traveller's Guide to Elizabethan
   England*, Bodley Head (2012) (Vintage edition, 2013)
Mantel, Hilary, *Wolf Hall*, Fourth Estate (2009)
Mantel, Hilary, *Bring up the Bodies*, Fourth Estate (2012)
Norris, Herbert, *Tudor Costume and Fashion*, Dover
   Publications (2007)
Penn, Thomas, *Winter King: The Dawn of Tudor Engl*
   Allen Lane (2011) (Penguin edition, 2012)
Starkey, David, *Monarchy*, Harper Press (2006)

If you enjoyed this book, you may also be interested in…

The House of Tudor
Alison Plowden

The Tudors ruled England for little more than a century, but no other dynasty has so impressed itself on the English consciousness. In a personal rather than political hi story, Alison Plowden tells the story of the five Tudor monarchs, as well as lesser-known members of the family. Superbly told, this is the story of four turbulent, passionate, tragic and prodigious generations.

978 0 7509 3240 0

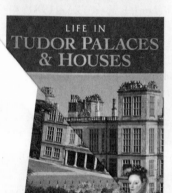

Life in Tudor Palaces & Houses
Alison Sim

Our nation is a treasury of outstanding palaces and fine merchant houses from this rich period in our past. Here we uncover what these remarkable buildings can tell us about Tudor lives and times: their daily routines; their diet and health; how they entertained themselves. This is an informative and entertaining look at the daily reality of life in the Tudor period, from the wealthiest families to the humblest of households.

978 1 84165 308 2